Kirby Soup for the Soul

WHITE HORSE BOOKS

This
one
is
for
Hallie.

R. K.

Kirby Soup for the Soul
copyright 2003 White Horse Books
all rights reserved
Printed in the United States

First Edition

9 8 7 6 5 4 3 2 1

library of congress lccn

ISBN 0-9744860-2-7

cover art and design Pat Bagley
editor Dan Thomas

Cartoonist's Note

Robert Kirby once told me he left police work for his health. Policemen, after all, suffer a higher than average incidence of alcoholism, depression, divorce and suicide. So a career change was in order.

He became a writer. A profession that is happily free of alcoholics, depressives, divorces and suicides.

Kirby actually left police work for other health reasons: his wife, Irene, said she would kill him if he didn't.

You see, in the millennium just gone by, Kirby was a veteran police officer in Springville, Utah. Rookie officers relied heavily on the fatherly, veteran cop. When coming upon a particularly nasty barroom brawl or ward basketball game, the rookies would call and prudently wait for Dad to show up and crack some heads. Kirby didn't mind. It was recreation.

Irene Kirby didn't share her husband's enthusiasm for bashing skulls (and occasionally having one's own creased). Instead, she encouraged in him a budding knack to crack people up with a pen rather than a night stick. So in a way, you have Irene to thank for this collection of Kirby columns taken from The Salt Lake Tribune. Included is the best of Kirby from the dawn of the twenty-first century.

If you don't think so, take it up with Irene.

— Pat Bagley

Kirby
Soup
for
the
Soul

Brand-New, Still-in-the-Box, Never-Been-Used, Millennium

The new millennium will be here in less than 48 hours. Judging from the run on bottled water, toilet paper and ammunition, many of you are making last minute party preparations.

A lot is supposed to happen when our clocks roll over (or don't) into the year 2000. Opinion seems fairly divided between three basic schools of thought:

- Widespread slow death caused by food shortages, financial panic and civil unrest.
- Widespread immediate death, caused by the Lord flash-frying the entire planet.
- Localized indifference, caused by one too many media references to Y2K.

For example, many religious fundamentalists are certain that this is the year when Jesus will come back and finally blow out the candles on his birthday cake. They predict nice things for those who agree with them, and horribleness for those who don't.

Conversely, most people see the upcoming trouble more as a mechanical problem. Namely, that some moron forgot to program computers with the ability to recognize the year

2000. The entire world will come to a halt at the stroke of midnight.

Yet others, myself included, believe that whatever problems do arise will occur primarily because people worried themselves silly over the change. When it comes to whether they are safe from the madness of Y2K, I worry less about my computer and toaster than I do about my neighbors. They're the ones with the guns and the paranoia.

If you are nervous about what's going to happen at midnight tomorrow to the extent that you just ran out and bought 4,000 cases of Playtex tampons and Ritz crackers, please take a deep breath.

Not everything that happens after midnight will be a sign that Y2K has arrived. Some of it, including really weird stuff, actually will be signs that nothing has changed except the fact that you've become a stress ninny.

For example, if you suddenly notice that you cannot call long distance after midnight, this does not mean that every telecommunication satellite in space has suffered a meltdown. More likely it's because every idiot on earth is trying to call somewhere to find out how their relatives are doing. The exact same thing happened last year.

If the streets seem eerily deserted at dawn on January 1, 2000, do not rush home and begin digging a bunker into your front lawn. It's a holiday, Mr. Wizard. Given the amount of celebrating that happened, chances are better than good that everyone is still asleep or in jail.

Do not be alarmed if you find some food items scarce immediately after 2000 A.D., including cocktail onions, margarita mix, olives, chips, etc. . . . It's just a temporary party problem.

If, however, you notice that stocks of flour, sugar, bottled water and disposable diapers are low, you can blame it on panic buying. These items will return to the stores once people wise up and start kicking themselves for trading their Krugerrands for pork and beans.

Odds are that a plane will crash somewhere in the world on January 1, 2000. Do not start telling yourself that it was a Y2K bug. Wait for the investigation to prove that it was, in fact, a combination of mountain and inattentive pilot.

Since most cars also have on-board computers, it may seem logical to interpret all the reckless driving after New Year's as a millennium problem. In truth, however, it has more to do with an age-old problem with alcohol.

Likewise, it may seem like the government has stopped working after Y2K. Rest easy. Our government actually stopped working in 1922. It's just your heightened sensibilities kicking in.

Finally, if you see a giant ball of fire in the east on New Year's Day, do not start looking around for your surplus army helmet. It isn't the Lord or a nuclear disaster. It's the sun.

Happy New Year.

We Are Still Here

The Millennium is four days old and the vast majority of us are still alive. Cool. Let's move from revolution to resolution with a bit more decorum, shall we?

For starters, we should probably think about how we're going to pay for all that survival stuff we cheerfully bought on credit when we didn't think there was going to be an American Express after Y2K.

Admit it, we were scared that a foreign mob would take control of our government, our money would become worthless, and we would have to defend our property from thieves and mercenaries.

The feared holocaust has become the equally dreaded hollercost. Meaning that the credit card companies are going to want their money a lot more than you still want those matching Glocks and 800 cases of pork and beans.

Think about it, Chicken Little. What are you going to do with a Model Gritz 50-gallon water purifier absolutely guaranteed to turn urine into Evian? The next Millennium scare is 999.9 years away.

If you weren't buying this stuff for yourself, someone else was buying it for you. Military surplus stores had a banner

Christmas season, as everyone tried to find the right gift for the well-armed family member.

This year, my mom bought me a first aid kit for my truck. It's small enough to put under the seat, which means that it contains enough stuff to treat a slightly injured gopher.

Noticeably lacking in the kit are any of the things I might need in an emergency of the collapsed civilization sort, namely, morphine, bone saw, Chapstick, adult diapers and a generous supply of Diet Coke.

In addition to this, I also received the following "sensible" Christmas gifts:

- Four 50-pound bags of wheat.
- A thousand rounds of slightly bent Mauser ammunition.
- Time-share on a mule.
- Urban-rubble-pattern, camouflage underwear.

Maybe survivors of the Y2K scare should have a swap meet. That way, we could recover some of the money we spent being afraid of something that didn't happen.

I could trade you my mule time-share for your automatic latrine digger. And you could offer me 2,000 freeze-dried bean dinners for half a case of smoke grenades and some night vision goggles.

You should be able to get at least $150, or a big sack of lizard jerky, for a large canvas tent complete with professionally installed firing slits. However, be careful when swapping donkeys for electrical generators. While it's true that you can get as many as five donkeys per generator, you can't play Nintendo with a donkey even if you have an adapter.

If you opt to sell rather than trade, please keep in mind that currency is risky in troubled times. You want precious metals instead of paper script. So, even though you were planning to turn your parents out into the wilderness for lack of food, you may want to hang onto them. Their dental work is like money in the bank.

Once we get our perspective (and possibly some of our money) back, we can start looking forward to the future without the paralyzing fear of the past few months. We can focus on a bright future.

Wait, I forgot about the Olympics. In two short years, life in Utah will come to an end. Our government will be controlled by foreigners. The average Utahn won't be able to afford anything, while thieves and mercenaries lock up all our services.

Forget the swap meet idea. It's important that we begin hoarding now.

Where's my VISA card? I'm going to need that automatic latrine digger more than ever now. Do you have any idea how much people will pay to go to the bathroom around here in 2002?

This Little Piggy Went To Milford

Recently, I mentioned the possibility of being sent to Milford on an undercover journalism assignment. The purpose of said trip: to determine where hot dogs really come from.

Although the whole hot-dog-origin-thing is a serious issue, I was just kidding around. It was like making an off-hand comment about being sent on assignment to the moon.

Some people have no appreciation for irony. This is part of what I was thinking as I drove into Milford early Friday morning. The other part was, "[expletive deleted] editor!"

Milford is a small farming/mining/something community located approximately 5,000 miles east of Japan. If you have to be there at 9 a.m., it's considerably further south from Salt Lake City.

About 1,500 people live and/or work in Milford. One of them is Brian Mauldwin, public affairs director for Circle Four Farms, the 17th largest pig farm in the country.

Brian was my contact for the undercover hot dog assignment. Since he knew I was a reporter, and everyone else in Milford knew that I didn't belong there, the undercover part didn't work all that well.

On our way out to one of 50 Circle Four pig farms, which turned out to be not in Milford, but instead almost to the Mexican border, Brian told me everything about pigs, including some stuff that may have violated my Constitutional rights.

Hog production is so effective that everything but a pig's "Oink!" has a commercial use. In addition to hot dogs, we also get water filters, cement, heart valves, cellophane, antifreeze, floor wax and legislative bills from pigs. Exactly which part of a pig is used to filter water, I cannot say, mainly because I threatened to kill Brian if he told me. He did say that while hot dogs come from many parts, all of these parts first had to come from an actual pig.

Making the actual pigs is what Circle Four does. There were about 500,000 pigs, each and every one of them made the old-fashioned way.

Me: Where did you get all these pigs?
Brian: Well, the father pig loves the mother pig very much, and then . . .

OK, what really happens is something called "artificial insemination," which you will have to take my word for, is way more shocking than where hot dogs come from.

I will say that I once believed I had the most embarrassing job in the whole world. Not anymore. My eyes have definitely been opened. In fact, I now have trouble sleeping.

The cool part of the process is when the piglets are born. At Circle Four Farms, "when" means every single minute of the day. In the time it took to write this, another 500 pigs were born.

Few things are cuter than a piglet. In one room, there were about 3,000 of them, all pink and cuddly and making Ned Beatty noises at the top of their lungs. It sounded just like C-Span.

Older pigs get transferred to large dormitory facilities, where they put on weight until the day they get shipped to Farmer John in California, who makes the actual hot dogs.

Because some controversy has been raised about the effects of an important pig by-product (manure), I should probably mention the smell.

There wasn't any.

Then we went into one of the pig barns and my hair spontaneously combusted.

After the tour, we went back to Milford for lunch. The waitress brought me a plate of pig feed as a joke. It tasted like unsweetened granola, but with the density of buckshot.

Driving out of Milford, I made several mental notes:

1) Do NOT find out what goes into hot dogs.
2) Tell the editor I was only kidding about the moon assignment.

Park City Film-flam Festival

Against my better judgement, I went to Park City yesterday and stalked some movie stars at the Sundance Film Festival.

I was hoping to get close to my film idol Homer Simpson, but he never showed. Ditto Marlon Brando, Donald Duck, O.J. Simpson, Elvira and Barney Rubble.

No problem. Park City still had more weird people per square inch than Roswell, New Mexico on a clear day. Everyone all full of themselves and yammering away on cell phones. "He's not an important, independent @*%#! film-maker! I'm a &#%*@ filmmaker with impact. It's about art, so where's my *&@% money?!"

It was impossible not to eavesdrop. Independent film makers of every hue, lingo, persuasion and political skew packed Main Street, hawking footage so avant-garde artsy that it might as well have been shot by Martians.

They had it all. If you wanted to locate a Pakistani remake of *The Alamo,* filmed on location at The Louvre, with Hopi subtitles, it was probably showing in the back of some guy's van.

A stroll down Park City's historic main drag resulted in a bale of handbills and leaflets announcing screening times. Trying to see the movies was another matter. All the good ones were sold-out.

I tried using my press credentials to get into a screening of, I swear, something like *Forty Crazy Presidents Riding Tiny Tricycles In Manure,* but was told to go away. Then some guy wanted me to watch a movie on his laptop, while another guy in a bear suit tried to hug me. The bear got away with this only because there were witnesses.

After an hour, I became annoyed (and not a little scared) and went looking for a familiar face. I found it at Cows, an ice cream parlor just down from the Egyptian Theater. Outside of Cows, Craig "Spike" Decker, of Spike & Mike's Sick and Twisted Festival of Animation, was handing out flyers. "Hi, I'm Spike. I'm famous and not a Mormon."

He almost had me with that line.

But it was the eyes on a movie poster behind Spike that drew me further in. I recognized those eyes. They were the famous eyes of Tammy Faye Bakker, former PTL queen and nationally televised weeper.

Back in the late '80s, Tammy and husband Jim ran the $100 million-a-year PTL church, until it collapsed from sexual scandal, fraud and spectacularly boring programming—even for a gospel show. Jim went to prison. Tammy became a recluse.

It was a long and sordid tale of woe made all the more unforgettable by Tammy Faye's trademark mascara leaking like the Exxon Valdez.

Flash forward to Park City, 2000. Tammy Faye Bakker Messner was in town to promote her newest film, *Through The Eyes of Tammy Faye*, a documentary tell-all about her life. The film is narrated by RuPaul Charles, famous cross-dresser.

Maybe it's just me. Does anyone else appreciate the irony of a movie about a woman who wears too much makeup being narrated by a guy who, since this is Utah, isn't supposed to be wearing any at all?

I had to check it out. There was a press conference going on inside Cows, so I went in and met Tammy Faye. I'm pleased to report that she was the most normal person in Park City on Wednesday. This includes the two cops whose presence kept me from punching the guy in the bear suit.

"I like Utah very much," Tammy told me. "It's so beautiful." [Please note that this is an actual quote. Not like the quotes that I sometimes make up, including the one about Michelle Pfeifer saying she wanted to marry me].

I got a free makeup kit from RuPaul and Tammy. It could be the start of a whole new me.

Love
Hurts

If you are a man, chances are you forgot that Monday is Valentine's Day. Now that you know, this seems a good time to pause for a large hysterical fit.

The angst you are feeling right now stems from a complete lack of understanding about what makes a woman feel romantic. I don't know either, so I looked it up on the internet. Not counting about 5,000 web sites that seem to correlate the word "romance" with "hot mamas," here's what I found out.

HOW TO ROMANCE A WOMAN:

> • Call her • Hug her • Compliment her • Smile at her
> • Laugh with her • Cry with her • Cuddle with her
> • Shop with her • Give her jewelry and flowers
> • Hold her hand • Write love letters to her
> • Go to the end of the earth and back again for her.

Conversely, if a woman wants to romance a man, she would only need to show up wearing anything remotely revealing, including a hazardous material suit.

This may sound like an over-simplification of gender romance differences, but it isn't far from reality. It's always Valentine's Day for men, if you get my drift. Women need a special day.

Because it involves a woman's feelings, Valentine's Day is something of a mystery to men. So is the top on a box of Cheeze Doodles, but we'll save that for another column.

The following is a basic guide to Valentine's Day survival for men, which was faxed to me by the nice ladies down at "Romance Anonymous," formerly known as "Men Are Pigs But We Can't Kill Them."

STEP ONE: The minimum requirement is to let the woman know that you care. The least expensive way is to look at her, preferably somewhere on her face, and say, "I love you, (her name here)." If you forgot her name, don't bother with the rest of the steps. You're dead.

STEP TWO: A Valentine card is an acceptable, non-verbal token of appreciation. Best of all, it's cheap. Good Valentines are pink, with lots of lace and cute words, like, "I'll love my sugar bunny forever and ever and ever and...." Bad Valentine cards say, "Good for one free quart of motor oil."

STEP THREE: Candy. For some scientific reason that makes no sense, women regard chocolate the same way men view beer. While a handful of M&Ms is OK, they tend to expect something a bit nicer. Wrapped, for starters.
(By the way, since the candy is supposed to be for her, she's going to notice any test bites. Stay out of it.)

STEP FOUR: Jewelry. A bit pricier, especially if you didn't bother with steps 1-3. If you did, you might get by with a small, but hideously expensive ring, necklace, or tiara. Keep in mind that most women, even in Utah, do not consider aluminum, tin or even a mylar balloon to be precious metals.

STEP FIVE: Lingerie. Be careful. Few men are smart enough about women to figure out their underwear. Not only does it have to be the right size and caliber, it must also match any of the approximately 8 billion feelings she currently has about herself. To be safe, tell the clerk that you're looking for something that can't be used to strangle you in your sleep.

STEP SIX: Romantic getaways are good for couples with more than .002 kids. Studies prove that not even bacteria can reproduce when a toddler is beating on the bedroom door with a Fisher-Price toy. Depending on the size of your family, the romantic getaway may have to cross at least three international boundaries.

STEP SEVEN: Unlike men, women give points for trying. So do something. Anything is better than nothing. If you don't believe me, I can show you last year's knot on the back of my head.

Sexy Beasts

If you noticed a large amount of hysterical noise coming from the direction of Hogle Zoo lately, you can relax. Word is that Cupid has been doing a little out-of-season hunting.

Zoo officials announced that its animal population is feeling extra frisky. Thanks to the warm weather, the zoo may soon expect a baby boom to rival BYU.

Actually, the announcement was made by *Tribune* reporter Lori Buttars, whose complete lack of zoology credentials is the main reason her Hogle Zoo romance story was printed without an R rating. Parts of her story were therefore censored for Utah County distribution.

According to the entire story, zoo animals are paying more than casual attention to each other. For example, polar bears Andy and Chinook are getting "reacquainted" after more than a year apart.

Big surprise. After a week, most humans would be lucky not to break a dozen laws and require the assistance of a chiropractor in the process of getting "reacquainted." A year apart is not romance, it's a lack of options.

This is not to say that we can't learn a great deal about romance from the animals. Virtually every method used by animals to attract mates is also used by humans. Except for the ones involving money, breast enhancement surgery and police decoys.

First, we can learn what not to do. For example, Breezy the wolf is ready for love. Unfortunately, her male companion, Dakota, has been castrated, which everyone knows is only next to excessive female leg hair in terms of inhibiting romance in males. Do not do this.

Another unromantic lesson comes to us from Mookie and Tino, the zoo's lowland gorilla pair. According to zoo officials, Mookie has allowed Tino to squeeze her posterior several times without immediately filing sexual harassment charges.

Unfortunately, Mookie has a history of throwing male suitors into the moat, the gorilla equivalent of a cold shower. Small wonder that she has yet to have any babies.

Officials claim that Mookie is becoming more receptive to male advances because she may hear her biological clock ticking. On the other hand, maybe that noise is just the sound of her beating on the skulls of the males.

We can also learn some important romance tips from the meerkat, a small mammal that looks as if God was making a weasel but changed his mind and made Ross Perot instead.

Meerkats have been highly romantic for no particular reason, other than the fact that they are locked in a cage together. It figures. Put male and female humans in a cage together and you get movies like *Chained Heat* and *Jail House Babes*.

Like humans, animals have learned to attract each other through smells, sounds and body language, all of which transmits to each other the subtle message, "Let's hurry up and do something we may regret a few months later."

A good example is snow leopards Dawa and Sherpa. Their keepers watch Dawa for signs that she is going into estrus, something that happens approximately every time Sherpa gets paid.

Typically, Dawa releases a scent (Eau de Fang, $35 a quarter ounce) that causes Sherpa's brain to short-circuit. He begins making a "chuffling" sound, which among human males is called "mouth breathing."

Later, Dawa and Sherpa get together in the middle of the night and make noises that cause humans as far away as Idaho to sit up in bed and exclaim, "Good lord, who set Aunt Vernice on fire?"

Later, when they are thinking more clearly, Dawa and Sherpa go directly over to the hyena cage to look for lawyers.

See? Exactly like humans, only without all the Valentine's Day fuss.

Main St. Blues

I am bored with the Main Street Plaza mess, which is what usually happens when attorneys and politicians try to resolve stuff by talking about it until one side or the other falls asleep.

For those who have not been paying attention to the plaza situation, perhaps a quick recap will help you understand how we got here.

1. The LDS Church buys a piece of Main Street from the city with the understanding that people will be allowed to come and go as they please.

2. A translation error soon reveals that the "they" actually refers to LDS Church security, which immediately boots people from the plaza for behavior ranging from skateboarding to hollering at the temple.

3. A bunch of court stuff happens, most of it boring and none of it followed half as closely as *American Idol*.

4. Each side of the issue (currently set at two dozen and counting) claims civilization will end if the U.S. Constitution is not interpreted in its favor.

My favorite observation so far comes from the Rev. Tom

Goldsmith of the First Unitarian Church. "If we can't find a peaceful solution for Main Street, is there any hope for Jerusalem?"

With all due respect to Tom, the answer is no.

The cantankerous mess in the Middle East got started exactly like this. Thousands of years ago, someone trod upon someone else's holy turf with a placard announcing, "The Lord of Hosts Says Beat It."

Today, news from that region does not contain boring shots of attorneys talking. It has pictures of Israeli tanks surrounding some guy who looks like a badger wearing a dish towel.

Pat Bagley and I have always wanted to be war correspondents and cover a really stupid conflict. Provided, of course, that we could go home every night. If the plaza thing turns into another Jerusalem, this could be it.

We immediately went down to Galyan's and bought matching safari jackets. While Pat put together his combat sketch artist kit, I worked on my war correspondent prose. See what you think:

Dateline: Somewhere in the Main Street Gaza Strip.

"In the eerie gloom, Mormon tanks grind cautiously through the bullet-pocked rubble. They pause only to fire 155-mm rubber bullets at rock-throwing ACLU street urchins.

"Earlier today, an army spokesman claimed the projectiles were nonlethal, but so far we have only been able to locate and interview the shoes of those struck by them.

"As we prepare to leave for another briefing, a prolonged detonation rocks the plaza. Someone running past shouts that Bible students have just dynamited the 'blasphemous' Eagle Gate statue of Brigham Young.

"In another part of the city, the enclave of the ACLU has

been surrounded by Mormon troops, who are pestering the leader into surrendering by playing 'We Thank Thee O God for a Prophet' nonstop from loudspeakers.

"No one knows when it will end. This recent outbreak of violence has continued to escalate ever since Mayor Rocky Anderson proposed a peaceful solution and was promptly gunned down by both sides.

"The situation here is tenuous. Unnerved by the constant shelling, Bagley has eaten all of our rations and some of his Crayolas."

Seriously, folks, please settle this plaza stuff before it turns into something so stupid that even I could win a Pulitzer covering it.

Can You Supersize That Humor Columnist?

If you are anything like me—and your mom would refuse to show her face in public if you were—winter has not been kind to you.

Over the past few months, you have let yourself go. You've gained weight, lost muscle tone and developed a deep root system from your butt down into a sofa.

Perhaps you had to buy an entirely new wardrobe, or screamed when you suddenly saw a hippopotamus in the mirror. In extreme cases, your belly button may have even become large enough to yodel into.

Spring is coming. I do not come by this information from any television weather forecasters on TV, who typically divine seasonal changes by shaking a bag of cat bones.

No, spring is coming because, well, it always does. It's now officially March. In just 19 more days, it will be officially spring, except in Park City and Alta, where they operate on winter savings time until July.

What this means is that the day is coming when you can finally leave your house in a pair of shorts, and you will want that glorious day to be marked by something other than a hor-rified neighbor taking a shot at you.

Fortunately, there is still time to begin a comprehensive exercise and diet program at least a hundred times before you finally give up and have all the openings in your head sewn shut.

Several months ago, a gym opened near my home. My wife suggested that we join. Although she said it late at night, behind closed doors, and spoken in barely a whisper, it was still loud enough to cause every gym between here and Tokyo to begin calling us.

"Lose 300 pounds for just $9,000," said one. Another promised us that if we didn't lose six inches off our waist-lines in 12 weeks, it would replant all the lost rainforest.

We joined the gym closest to our house. That was two weeks ago, and I've since recovered enough muscle tone to open my own Doritos bags. I don't pass out when I try to see my feet and my heart no longer sounds like a belt sander.

If I can do it, so can you. All it takes is money, time, masochism and a loved one's nonstop reminders that you look stupid using a garden hose for a belt.

Initially, a gym is a frightening and confusing place. Not only is it full of people already in shape, but also contains a great deal of machinery once the property of Nazi Germany.

For example, there's the Lateral Pull-Down Triceratops Strangulator that, should the name alone fail to scare you off, will pull your spine clear out of your pelvis if you use it wrong.

So always seek professional help from a responsible and unfeeling trainer. The guy who helps me at my gym is Jim. Jim can do 50-pound curls with his uvula.

Jim is serious. When he asked what my goals were, I said I would be happy if I could just cut back on the amount of cellulite on my forehead. Jim didn't laugh.

According to Jim, it's most important not to overdo exercise, thereby running the risk of injury and discouragement. Start out low and slow, and gradually work your way up to a point where you no longer crawl back to your car.

Never compare yourself to other people in the gym. Everyone there is on a different level, including the lone, pathetic chub that you feel superior to, until you realize that it's you in a mirror.

More than anything else, you should keep going. After all, you paid for a gym membership that you have to keep paying for even if you stop using it. That's like paying for the privilege of staying fat.

Jury Rigged

I was in Fourth District Court yesterday. This time, however, they wanted something from me other than a fine. I got this threatening letter notifying me for jury duty. Among other things, the letter explained a variety of official evils that might befall me should I fail to cooperate fully with the jury process.

Although not yet officially called, I went to the courthouse to see if a judge would really throw me in jail for not showing up. Let the record show, "Oh, yeah."

We won't get into the irony of incarcerating me for refusing to help incarcerate someone else. The point is that if you go to court in Utah County, you may see me sitting in the jury box. Do not get your hopes up.

I filled out the "Juror Qualification Questionnaire," which, when spoken rapidly, can actually be used as a field sobriety test. The questionnaire wanted to know what language I spoke, where I was from and was I a convicted felon?

Taking special notice of the word "convicted," I was able to answer all the questions in such a way that I probably qualify to be called.

Not everyone is this cooperative. Lots of people don't want to be on a jury. Part of the problem is that trials take forever. Jurors on high profile cases sometimes have children they've never seen.

Then there's the matter of money. Jury duty pays $18.50 for the first day, which works out to be well below minimum wage in the Congo. It gets better the second day ($49), and every day thereafter, including the day you finally go insane from boredom.

Anyway, that's why at the very bottom of the form is a place to plead for being excused. It isn't a big space, so you have to be very creative. Do not write, "Because I will bring a bomb to court," in this space.

I used this handy space to write, "I triple-dog dare you to call me for jury duty."

I can do this because even if they call me, there's no way I will get to be on a jury. I'd still have to get through the screening process, wherein attorneys for both sides get to pick the jury.

It works like this. They cram a bunch of sullen, prospective jurors into the courtroom and allow attorneys to ask questions regarding their ability to be objective.

Attorneys are good at asking questions. They are even better at jumping up and shouting, "Objection!" They will do this if a prospective juror says something completely unconstitutional, such as, "Damn right O.J. was guilty."

I've spent enough time in court to know that there is no way I would get through this process. Lawyers hate prospective jurors like me. For starters, I used to be a cop. Cops believe everyone is guilty of something. This includes all your friends, your mom, your attorney, the rest of the jury and especially all religious leaders.

Next, I have already formed an opinion on whatever it is that you are alleged to have done, even if it's more complicated than I could possibly figure out. That's the journalist part of me.

Then there's the little matter of being tried by a jury of your peers. Sorry, but anyone who seriously believes that I'm one of their peers definitely belongs in jail.

Finally, I believe in the death penalty. I don't care if it's a dog custody case, somebody is going to be orbiting the earth when we get done. You can't waste everyone's time and get away with just a slap on the wrist.

But if I do get called, I will serve proudly. It's my duty as an American. Plus, you can always appeal.

Erin go Beehive

Tomorrow is St. Patrick's Day. If stereotypes are your thing, by now you have painted yourself green, drank yourself half into oblivion, and picked a fight with anyone remotely British looking.

Quit it. This is not the way to celebrate St. Paddy's Day. For one thing, punching people who look even a wee bit like Queen Elizabeth would include many Germans. Do not do this. For another, getting horrendously drunk and passing out face-down in a toilet is no more Irish than it is Scottish, English, Welsh or even Tooele-nish. Wait for Journalism Day.

I don't know about painting yourself green. That part could be Irish. No one else ever does it. Knock yourself out.

Unfortunately, most people are introduced to erroneous Irish customs while still in grade school. For example, anyone not wearing green on St. Patrick's Day got pinched, typically until they almost bled to death internally.

In my fourth grade class, a kid named Leon ran around pinching everyone, regardless of what they were wearing. We thought he was mentally ill, but it turned out that he was just color-blind.

So, customs and traditions can sometimes get out of hand. We don't want that to happen tomorrow, unless of course, you're British and simply can't help yourself.

If you want to celebrate St. Patrick's Day properly, pay attention. I am part Irish—the part that 150 years ago said, "Let's get the hell out of here and go to America." I will try and talk you through it.

First, a brief history lesson about the big day. It was named for St. Patrick, who, as legend has it, drove all of the snakes out of Ireland. Exactly how this was accomplished (or even why) is a mystery.

Even though Ireland is a huge island and therefore easy to find, the snakes never came back. Possibly they went to America, too. At any rate, there are no snakes in Ireland today. Instead, there are leprechauns.

Real leprechauns are nothing at all like the guy on the Lucky Charms box. Lucky resembles an actual leprechaun the same way that the Hamburgler resembles a real burglar. Your free range leprechaun is mean, ugly, greedy and nasty. The ones who immigrated to America went immediately into politics.

Despite what you may see tomorrow, the Irish do not use a lot of Green Dye #4 when they cook. Forget green eggs, green spuds and green beer. Traditional Irish food consists of cabbage, potatoes and something called corned beef.

Making real corned beef without a nuclear reactor is time consuming. Custom calls for a cow raised entirely on corn liquor, which is then cooked for about a year, beaten severely, and finally thrown from a really tall cliff. What pieces you find practically melt in your mouth.

A more mythological Irish tradition is kissing the blarney stone. Blarney is an ancient Celtic word meaning "campaign promise" or "fine print." Researchers aren't exactly sure.

To kiss the actual blarney stone requires going to Ireland, finding the popular tourist site of Blarney Castle, and kissing a stone worn smooth by 500+ years of tourist lips. Those who do this are supposedly rewarded with persuasive speech, as well as three types of hepatitis.

All the Irish language you need to know tomorrow is "Erin go Bragh." This is an ancient Irish phrase meaning "Erin went outside to throw up." It will come in handy if someone asks you where Erin went.

If you want to look Irish tomorrow, pin some shamrocks to your lapels. A shamrock is a form of grass that closely resembles the suit of clubs in a deck of cards. It's also a club.

The important thing to remember is that everyone is Irish on St. Paddy's Day. Well, maybe not Queen Elizabeth.

Waging Wasp War

Today is the first day of spring, and already I lost a fight with a bug. On Saturday, while serving a completely legal eviction notice on a wasp nest in my tool shed, one of them stung me.

Getting stung only started the fight. It made me mad, so I took a swing at the nest with a shovel. I missed and knocked a drill box off the shelf, which landed on my foot.

One thing led to another. I got stung again. There's a ragged hole in the wall where the nest was, and numerous five-pound wads of latex caulk sealing individual wasps to various parts of the shed. My drill is broken and I'll probably lose a toenail.

As bad as this brawl went, it's still better than the year I rounded up 500 wasps with a Shop Vac. Being a novice wasp fighter then, I removed the lid without first tossing in a grenade. Regular wasps are humanitarians compared to spin-cycled wasps.

It's not just me. Now that spring is here, fights with wasps will be breaking out all over the state. If you want to win these fights, or at least break even, I have some important wasp-fighting tips.

These are legal tips from actual experts. I got them by going to the Utah State University Extension office in Provo and asking for karate lessons. They know me over there, and immediately asked what kind of bug beat me up this year.

According to these so-called experts—who I suspect may be idiots—wasps are beneficial "because they feed on caterpillars, beetle larvae, flies and other insects."

I don't care about any of that, and neither should you. These are violent bugs with almost zero ability to discern between Larry Erdmann and a large beetle larva.

The good news is that it's not yet against the law to kill wasps, hornets, yellow jackets, or even the more common "giant [expletive deleted] with huge stingers."

For purposes of killing, please do not confuse the common honeybee with wasps. Bees are good. They belong to a union. Without them, there would be no expensive Honey Nut Cheerios.

NOTE: Do not confuse regular bees with killer bees, which scientists tell us are bees that have joined a gang.

There are solitary wasps and social wasps. Solitary wasps are mud daubers. They construct tube-like nests of mud under eaves and in attics, and inside swamp coolers. Being loners, they aren't as dangerous.

Social wasps are the ones that build paper nests out of back issues of the *Tribune*. There's a nest under my deck the size of a hot air balloon. It's full of angry terrorist hornets.

According to the USU extension paper on wasp removal, I should "initiate control by destroying the nest." Makes sense, but I would like to point out that the same article noticeably fails to add, "without being killed in the process."

The easiest way is to squirt the nest with an insecticide. Do this at night, when all the wasps are home. You don't want a bunch of wasps coming home tired from the office and find you on their property.

Another way, perhaps even the stupidest way (not counting the Shop Vac method), is to knock the wasp nest down. To do this safely, you will need to clad yourself in protective gear. A tank is nice.

Once the nest is down, do not pick it up and hold it to your ear to see if the wasps inside want to surrender. Assume that they do not.

Once the nest is gone, you can prevent future wasp infestations by getting rid of the things that attract them. Since the number one thing wasps like is human skin, consider remaining indoors until next winter.

Dodge Ball Boogie

This is me in 5th grade: 41 pounds, half of which was the lenses in my glasses. This is what a dodge ball victim looked like in 1962.

For those who missed the dodge ball experience in school, it works like this. Kids choose up sides and face each other over a line. Then they hurl balls at each other. If you get hit, you're out. Eventually, one side wins.

Dodge ball had other names, including "murder ball," "slaughter ball," "cannon ball," and at Park Lane Elementary, "Bobby ball," in honor of the easiest (and most preferred) kid to hit.

Because it was a core class back then, I took dodge ball every year. Sometimes I took dodge ball in the legs and stomach. More often than not I got it in the head, which seemed to be the slowest part of me even back then.

Because I was slow, small, weak and generally clueless, I fared poorly at dodge ball.

I came home once and showed the old man my glasses, still missing a lens that wouldn't be found until the janitor swept behind the bleachers.

"Dodge more," my dad said.

Good advice. Possibly even the most workable advice a kid like me ever got on a school subject.

More than getting yelled at by teachers, dodge ball taught me that there were times when daydreaming could be a serious liability.

For example, if Eddie Manakea had the ball, and I was suddenly overcome with the distracting thought of kissing Becky Sanderson on the monkey bars, chances of the school nurse taking me home early went way up.

A lot of kids will be missing the educational experiences afforded by dodge ball. Granite and Salt Lake school districts have banned it. National groups are lobbying against it.

According to its detractors, dodge ball reinforces negative behavior such as aggression, violence, and just plain meanness. It's the food chain at it's worst, and can make school unpleasant for kids who look like the one at the top of this column.

The logic I guess is to remove this potentially damaging experience from the lives of weaker and slower kids. Everything will be rosier if kids don't have to face environments not specifically suited for their skills.

Frankly, if school was looking to remove potentially injurious activities from my curriculum, I would have much preferred they remove the one that says ugly kids don't get to date cheerleaders.

It would also have been nice if the football team had needed a center with the size and muscle density of a half blind, malnourished chicken.

And let's not forget the completely unfair grading system. If lazy and stupid kids can't do just as well on the SAT, we should get rid of it.

Maybe not. As painful as it was, I'm thinking that dodge ball taught me more about real life than anything else I took in school.

For one thing, you can only hide behind slower and stupider people for so long. When they get drilled, you need a better plan than simply pretending to be invisible.

There are worse things than being chose last. Getting hit first is one. The throwers' arms are fresher.

Leading a charge is way more dangerous than leading a retreat.

Do not lose your cool. Panic is merely the illusion of being faster and smarter.

Prayer works more often in the Bible than it ever does during stuff like dodge ball, military draft, job lay-offs and the lottery.

When the odds are against you, keep your thoughts to yourself. Mercy is never wasted on loudmouths.

If you can choose, getting it in the legs is better than getting it in the head. Legs heal. Glasses cost money.

Dad Gummed Gummint

I spent most of last week in Washington, D.C. I went there to do some investigative journalism on the workings of our government. Here's what I found out.

There is no government. Not in any form that resembled what you and I sometimes refer to in our wildest dreams as "common sense."

Our nation's capitol reminded me of a trip I once made to Mars, which I believe occurred in 1972. Bammer, however, still insists that we were simply drunk and in Las Vegas.

The point is that I ate several airline meals containing 580 percent of the recommended daily requirement of polyurethane, to find out that Washington, D.C. would be a great place for a nuclear test range.

When I arrived, a large crowd of under-medicated idiots seemed to think they were in charge. What looked like dress down day at a badly kept zoo turned out to be a demonstration against something called the World Bank.

For those unfamiliar with the World Bank, it's the same outfit that First Security Bank tried to merge with several years ago, a move that cost a billion dollars and ended 20 minutes after it started an ear-biting brawl over parking validation.

It was right out of <u>The Hobbit</u>. On one side was an army of nasty orcs (police). On the other was a disturbing array of ill-bathed elves, gnomes and gremlins (demonstrators).

Caught squarely in the middle were a huge number of camera-toters who just wanted to see the Lincoln Memorial.

Both sides had vastly different agendas. The police wanted to keep the roads open and World Bank folk unlynched. The demonstrators wanted . . . well, it depended on which one you talked to, what time of day it was, and your astrological sign.

Demands ranged from protecting the rain forest to total anarchy. According to one demonstrator, anarchy was "the ability to do as you please as long as you don't harm anyone."

This, of course, is the precise definition of anarchy when you look it up in the <u>Big Book Of Drugs</u>. For the rest of us, anarchy means a complete loss of government control.

Fortunately for the demonstrators, there was a lot of government control. When they blocked streets, the cops kept them from being run over by livid commuters, who knew what real anarchy meant and wanted some of it for however long it took them to get to work.

There was surprisingly little violence, though both sides repeatedly hollered foul. Cops claimed that demonstrators manufactured their own chemical weapons and had stockpiles of rocks and bottles.

Demonstrators said cops (referred to as "corporate servants") deprived them of their rights by using pepper spray and clubs whenever they attempted to deprive other people of their rights.

This mainly amounted to demonstrators preventing people

from free access to public places. At one blockade, a group of girls locked arms and prevented disinterested pedestrians from proceeding.

"People have tried to get past us," said one activist calling herself Starshine, "but they failed."

Since Starshine had the muscle density of a gecko, my guess is that no one tried very hard.

As both a former cop and former demonstrator, I've been in half a dozen demonstrations and two certified riots. But I've never been in one where both sides were so pleased with themselves at the outcome.

Approximately 1,300 demonstrators submitted to voluntary arrest, happy to have struck a blow for freedom without getting struck themselves. Conversely, the cops didn't have to shoot anyone and they pulled down $5 million in overtime. Meanwhile, the rest of America waited for it to be over, cleaned up the mess, and then trudged to work to pay for it.

Larry, Curley & Mower

There was a time when human beings lived closer to the earth. I believe it was the Starvassic Period, approximately 15 million years before the evolution of the urban lawn.

It was a simpler time for men. Nobody cared if we killed stuff, didn't bathe, or even that an angry god called Big Ralph sometimes required that we hurl our mother-in-laws from a cliff.

Then some idiot invented the two-stroke gasoline engine. Civilization soon appeared in the form of a lawnmower. Thereafter, man was expected to hang around the house on Saturday and cut the grass.

Early man did not take to lawn mowing as easily as you might think. Complete civilization had to wait until early woman figured out that early man was lying whenever he said, "I'll be back in a minute."

This, of course, is a condensed history of the domestication of man. I left out a bunch of stuff, including the Peloponnesian Wars, golf, helmet laws and unemployment insurance.

Today, the results are everywhere. Large numbers of sweating men push loud contraptions across the same land we once roamed free, and were sometimes stomped flat by mastodons.

Not everything has changed. Each spring, modern man must still contend with a dangerous and wily beast, whose natural function it is to spring from ambush and say, "Just where in hell do you think you're going?"

Seconds later, man finds himself out in the garage/shed, cursing Big Ralph and yanking on the starting cord of a Toro. Said yanking continues until the engine starts or man's heart quits.

Lucky is the man whose mower starts right up. If it doesn't, some form of maintenance is required. Lamentably, the word "maintenance" makes no more sense to modern men than does the word "maturity."

So, we guess. When the mower doesn't start, we kick it. Then we take out the spark plug, spit on it, squirt some starter fluid inside the engine, and quickly replace the plug. Repeat yanking.

If the spark plug doesn't shoot out and kill someone, it's safe to begin. Not that mowing is safe, of course. Dollar for dollar, your basic lawn mower remains the best personal injury device in America.

Most mowers operate on the principle of a large blade spinning around fast enough to chop grass and pulverize sprinkler heads. If you stick your toes under there, it will chop them too. Ditto the wife's toy poodle, but don't tell her you got the idea from me.

It's important to keep the blade sharp. Sucking 90 feet of steel dog chain into a mower reduces grass cutting to vague theory. Thereafter, mowing the lawn constitutes more of a beating than an actual cutting.

Aside from gasoline mowers, there are two other forms of cutting the grass: electrical and the unspeakably heinous manual mower (invented by medieval, flagellate monks).

An electrical lawn mower starts right up, but requires one of two things. Either that you pay attention to where the cord is at all times, or you own a large supply of electrician's tape.

CAUTION: before repairing the cord, disconnect it from the outlet. Failure to do so may result in a personal message from Big Ralph that goes in your finger and simultaneously out a certain bodily orifice rarely mentioned in Sunday school.

The manual mower has an external power source as well. You. Consequently, it takes about nine days to cut a quarter-acre lawn with one of these.

None of these vegetation removal methods is as effective as the one early man was completely satisfied with before early woman got so much say. Namely, fire.

Alas, the old ways are gone for good. At least that's what the fire department just got done telling me. On the bright side, they did water what was left of the lawn.

Dog Dazed

On Saturday, my two dogs, Zoe and Scout, dug a hole in our tomato planter all the way past Hell and up through Pakistan.

That isn't the bad part. When the crime was discovered, they lied about it. Covered with mud and dirt, they hunkered fearfully at the bottom of the steps with their ears flat and said, "The cat did it."

So, I beat the cat.

Actually, I only thought about beating Bob Valdez. Ever since Bob got a restraining order because of the gopher-in-the-sock-drawer incident, I haven't been allowed to get within 50 feet of him.

This illustrates a fundamental problem with owning pets. People believe everything their pets tell them, especially dogs. Dogs have a secret brain ray that alters human thought.

It works like this. Say you're thinking about the national economy, when struck by an overwhelming urge to buy your dog a McDonalds Extra Value Meal. Racing out the door, you can't escape the feeling that you need to super-size it. And buy some tennis balls.

OK, stop for a minute. Look around. Notice the dog staring at you from the hallway? That brown-eyed gaze is not a look of adoration. It's the dog's brain ray in action.

Now go. We'll finish the rest of this column when you get back.

Scientists have known about the dog brain ray for years. They kept it a secret because there is no known antidote. People who have dogs go hopelessly crazy.

According to several studies, we also live longer, happier lives than people who do not have pets. I am not sure about snake owners here. Whether or not they live longer probably depends on the size of the snake.

All of this is important right now because of the giant Animal Adoption Fair held in Salt Lake City over the weekend. Hundreds of people abandoned their fates to dogs and cats.

Unfortunately, thousands more animals will be put to sleep because they couldn't find humans to control.

If you are one of the people who adopted a dog over the

weekend, or you are simply considering an adoption, there is a way to lessen the effects of this brain ray.

NOTE: Cats do not have a secret brain ray. They get what they want through cunning, stealth and lawyers.

The first step in coping with mind control by a dog is in knowing that it is occurring. If there is a dog within 50 feet of you right now, it's happening.

Stop reading that stuff right now.

The dog may appear to be lying innocently at your feet, but its mind it still working. If the tail moves, it's working really hard.

We need to go for a walk.

Dogs are known for being hysterically happy when their owners come home, or when their owners simply make eye contact with them. This is simply a way of getting humans to lower their guard.

And chase some cats.

When your guard is down, the dog will sit patiently and fix you with a look of utter devotion. Actually, he or she or it is staring at a spot on your forehead where the skull is the thinnest.

I have to go to the bathroom on the bishop's lawn.

You can fight against this mind control by forcibly directing your thoughts to stuff like the trade deficit, rising oil prices, changes in the Republican party, or simply imagining John Goodman in a Speedo.

And then we can buy some wieners.

There's some more stuff, but I . . . need to go dig in the tomato planter.

Right now.

A Kolob By Any Other Name

Back in the days when I was a Boy Scout (41 days to be exact), our scoutmaster, Ray Buckwaller, took us camping to a beautiful place high in the mountains. It was called Whorehouse Flats.

Ray didn't tell us the name of the place. We learned it from a sign on the dirt road leading into what was once an old mining camp. When we asked him what it meant, Ray hedged until we became suspicious.

"Remember when I took you guys to the county fair?" he said. "And there was that girl in a booth selling kisses for a dollar? It's like that, only worse."

Later that night, while Ray slept off the effects of fighting the forest fire we accidentally set, Harold Price explained the name in such shocking detail that most of us vowed to never get married.

Infatuated by the evilness of the name, we repeated it at length throughout the remainder of the weekend. By the time we left, it had lost its shock value.

When we got home, the bishop's son told his dad that Ray took us "up to that whorehouse place," where we had a blast until the forest rangers showed up. Shortly thereafter (about an hour), Ray was released.

I went back to Whorehouse Flats five years ago. It was still beautiful, but now the sign read, "Heavenly Meadow." Asking around, I learned that the flats had fallen under the scrutiny of people with tender sensibilities, who had the name changed to something less offensive.

They weren't satisfied with a slight alteration either. None of this "Floozie Flats" or "Hussy Haven." They went all the way.

The name changers are now eyeing Squaw Peak above Provo, insisting that the word "squaw" is derogatory enough to Native American women that it warrants changing.

Some words just summon the wrong images. No one knows this better than advertisers. That's why you probably (and mercifully) will never see a gourmet ice cream marketed by the name of Ben & Jerry's Explosive Gorilla Diarrhea.

But when it comes to name changes, the big question is how far you let other peoples' tender sensibilities go before the word "proper" brings to mind the image of a bunch of weenies?

Hopefully, it's long before some nitwit moves to change Crazy Bob Creek to "Mentally Challenged Robert Waterway," or Deadhorse Point to "Animal Abuse Promontory."

In these days of easy offense, it's only a matter of time before someone demands that religious place names be removed from government maps. Here in Utah, such separation of church and state would take forever.

In the interest of an easier transition, please consider the following relatively accurate substitutions to local Mormon place names.

NEPHI — Town in Juab County named for character in The Book of Mormon. Remove the offensive religious connotation by changing to a randomly selected, given name, such as "Bill."

MORONI — Another town in Juab County and gold figure with trumpet atop many LDS temples. Suggested change: "Hornblowerville."

LEHI — Yet another Book of Mormon character. Change to "Micronton."

MANTI — Famous lately for religious polygamy sect. Change to "Bigamy City."

KOLOB — Canyons in Iron and Washington counties. Also LDS reference to where God resides. Change to "Non-denominational Canyon."

BRIGHAM CITY — Named for Brigham Young. Change back to original "Box Elder." Change again for ageist reasons to just plain "Box."

DIRTY DEVIL RIVER — Change to "Unclean Spirit River."

LA VERKIN — Anglo corruption of Spanish "la Virgen," or the Virgin Mary. Change to "La Gherkin."

ZION CANYON — "Public Transportation Canyon."

ST. GEORGE — Remove "Saint." From now on, it's just "George."

WASATCH MOUNTAINS — Indian word meaning (loosely), "Hey, let's be nice to these Mormons and see what happens." Change to "Keep on going Mountains."

Mother of All Holidays

For Mother's Day, I tried to talk my mother into going to Washington, D.C. for the Million Mom March. She wouldn't go. It's too bad. With her exemplary mother record, she could make a difference in the nation's capitol.

Any woman who can bring several borderline sociopaths into the world and browbeat all of them into graduating high school without suffering a stroke must have some serious mom juju.

My mind (such as it was) seemed an open book. She cuffed me on the head the first time she caught me staring at the new neighbor girl. And she knew before the police that it was me who built the infamous manure gun.

When she came home and found a hole blasted through the garage door, she knew right away that it wasn't the Jehovah's Witnesses who put it there. Ditto the goat on our roof.

I realized later that Mom had no special ability to read the adolescent male mind. She was just married to my dad.

Being a mom is a highly under-appreciated job. I didn't

understand this until I became a father. This enabled me to objectively monitor the process of molding small forms of evil into responsible adults.

For starters, my kids wouldn't have lived very long without their mother. Not only does the mom know important health stuff, but it's never even occurred to her that children make excellent lode testers when wiring the house.

Forget basic safety. Let's talk medicine. Unlike fathers, moms have this uncanny ability to recognize that penicillin works better against strep throat than a bag of Popsicles and a kung fu movie.

Moms also seem better at nutrition. Sometimes they may get very angry if, while they are gone for a week, you feed your kids only pancakes and root beer. Pretending that you never heard of scurvy or rickets doesn't make the mom any happier.

Hygiene is also a mom function, although the logic they use for it makes no sense to most fathers. There is a perfectly good reason why a father can shoot and gut an elk, but cannot change a messy diaper. Scientists simply haven't discovered what it is yet.

I found out that it takes a mom to adequately (meaning that someone won't call the police) clothe a small child. In our house, this was the only reason why Saran Wrap never became an acceptable alternative to rain coats and galoshes.

Likewise, it's the mom that keeps the dad from making a girl wear a converted oil drum to school shortly after she hits puberty. Even if the dad swears this is the best way to keep him from killing the boys that will start following her home.

It's not long before kids realize that mom has special powers dad will never possess, like patience and long-suffering. If a kid drives the family car into a canal, they almost always want the mom to show up first.

Children soon learn to rely on these special mom powers to get what they want. They stop asking, "Dad, can we go to the movies tonight?" and start saying, "Mom says get in the car."

Finally, a mom is what it takes to make some kids get out of bed and go to school. Sometimes by saying, "Do you want to end up writing for a newspaper like your father?"

Looking back, it's obvious that I owe the moms in my life a lot. That's why I got them both a chain saw for Mother's Day.

Being moms, even if they hate it they'll let me keep it.

That's the Ticket

Got a speeding ticket west of Duchesne on Friday. Yet another innocent motorist set upon by the forces of darkness. You've heard of Rodney King? Well, now there's Robert Kirby. Here's what happened:

I was minding my very own business—which just happened to involve driving Warp Factor 9 on Highway 40—when suddenly my wife spoke up.

"Trooper," she said.

"Oh, [shoot]," I said.

Sure enough, there was a Utah Highway Patrol car coming toward us. As we passed each other, the patrol car's brake lights came on. Knowing that I was toast, I pulled over and waited.

The trooper was Jeffrey B. Chugg, #328. I would like to state for the record that he cursed me, dragged me out, pistol-whipped me, and then shot me in the leg for good measure. All while I pleaded for an expensive lawyer.

Unfortunately, none of this happened, but it certainly makes for a more interesting column. What's the world coming to when getting stopped by the police isn't a horrible experience?

What really happened is that Chugg—nice as pie and about 12 years old—wrote me a ticket, thanked me for wearing my seat belt, and sent me on my way.

This contrasts highly with the last two times I got pulled over, both times by former co-workers, who actually did call me names and threatened to shoot me if I didn't slow down.

I thought about contesting the ticket. My cunning defense would have rested entirely on the scientific fact that it's impossible to drive the speed limit when "Back in the USSR" by the Beatles is playing.

I decided to give Chugg the break he didn't give me. Besides, knowing what I know about rural justices, there's every reason to believe the judge would have thrown me in jail for wasting his time.

Also, I deserved the ticket (and about 500 others that I never got because no one was looking). I am a horrible driver. Despite the fact that I was once a cop and wrote thousands of tickets to other people for the same stuff, I routinely speed, fail to stop, change lanes improperly, and exercise poor lookout. Oh, and sometimes I let my dog steer while I look at the map.

Actually, judging from what I see on the way to work, this pretty much makes me an average Utah motorist. Meaning that a blind, deaf, rabid chimpanzee is a better insurance risk.

Part of the problem is the condition of the road. For example, have you tried driving the speed limit on I-15 through Salt Lake? That isn't a commute. It's a pursuit. You stand a better chance of obeying the speed limit after your parachute fails to open.

These days, one guy with a flat tire can paralyze northern

Utah. So, I drive fast on the freeway because I know that it's only a matter of time before the next traffic jam.

Here's the math for that: The faster you drive on the freeway correlates to spending less time on the freeway, which in turn significantly reduces the odds of spending large amounts of time on the freeway at 0 mph.

NOTE: This defense does not work on most troopers, who work the math this way: A+B+C=UHP or ($50 for 80 mph in a 65 mph zone).

Mainly, though, I think speeding is more a state of mind. Each and every one of us thinks we're more special than whatever is going on around us. We don't think the rules apply to us, so we cut corners whenever possible.

Apparently, this is a real problem for me. When I tried to add the fine for the speeding ticket on today's expense report, the editor said, "Not so fast, pal."

Man Walks Into a Bar . . .

I tended bar at Murphy's Bar & Grill last Thursday, eight hours of serious investigative journalism only slightly more confusing than last year's foray into artificially inseminating pigs.

Being a non-drinker, it seemed important that I familiarize myself with the impending fiasco of alcohol service during the Olympics. The staff and regulars at Murphy's were gracious enough to teach me.

Here is what I found out: bartending is harder than it looks in the movies. It's also more complicated than air traffic controlling, which I haven't tried yet, but it just has to be.

In the movies, a bartender mostly just wipes the bar with a rag and periodically gets shot for opening his mouth at the wrong time.

A cowboy never swaggers into a movie bar and says, "Gimme your best Silk Panties, barkeep." Not unless he's got some serious lace on his lariat.

There are—and I'm pretty close here—three-quarters of a million different kinds of liquor, and half again as many beers and wines. From these it's possible to make an array of drinks that would stretch from here to the end of a Supreme Court decision.

So the margin for error is huge. Fortunately, I had competent teachers in the form of Murphy's mixologists Alan and Chip. After tying on an apron, I was ready for my first customer.

A highly attractive woman came into the bar and said, "Would you make me a Godchild?"

I said, "Sorry, I'm married."

This was the wrong answer, and during the Olympics it might have caused an international incident with the Italians. Alan smoothed things over by showing me how to mix a Godchild, which, believe it or not, is just like a root beer float but with booze.

This turned out to be one of the easier drinks to make. Please do not ask me to remember what goes into a Colorado Bulldog, a Vulcan Mind Probe, or a '57 T-Bird with Honolulu License Plates.

Mostly I made screwdrivers, Bloody Marys, martinis, and something called a samurai. Then while customers drank, I listened to complaints about bad bosses, worse spouses, the government and Utah's bizarre liquor laws.

It's not enough to know what goes into drinks like a Brain Hemorrhage, or a Flying Kangaroo. A bartender also has to be a good listener for the simple reason that the noise level in even a moderately popular bar is worse than an LDS Primary meeting.

It helps if you can reads lips, but only until about 11 p.m., when customers' lips and most of the rest of their faces seem to become partially paralyzed.

Because of this, I paid close attention to the possibility of over-serving people, something we never did at Murphy's. Over-serving refers to giving more drink to people who have obviously had too much.

For some people, this could be a single drink. Alcohol, even in moderate amounts, can transform normally nice people into complete wieners. SLOC should pay close attention to this fact if, presumably, France is going to be invited.

This is the reason why a bar needs competent (muscular) people working the doors. At Murphy's this was Ra and Tuffy. Ra was built like a SWAT van, and Tuffy gave my neck a charlie horse just by looking at it.

I cannot personally vouch for everyone making it home safe from Murphy's. I almost didn't make it home myself. When my shift ended at 1 a.m., it took a half hour to find a way to get on I-15. The Department of Transportation had closed all the on-ramps for construction.

Considering the complexity of bartending and Utah's liquor laws, this arrangement was probably just a big field sobriety test set up by the police.

Grayer Shade of Pale

Yesterday, my wife sent me to the hardware store for a can of gray paint. She might as well have asked for a prolonged and expensive divorce.

I've been married long enough to know better. But like an idiot, I asked, "What shade?"

I figured to be on safe ground. In the unsophisticated world of testosterone there are only two shades of gray, both of which clearly fall somewhere between black and white. There's light gray and dark gray. Simple.

"Get an off-gray," she said. "Maybe an off-off-gray. You know, like those flecks in Pierce Brosnan's eyes? Sort of a mysterious and sensual gray."

The paint was for a door jam. I figured I could wing it. Besides, there was no way I was asking the guy at the hardware store for anything sensual.

There were 311 different shades of gray paint at the hardware store. I use the word "different" very lightly (or darkly) here, because the only way to tell some of the shades apart was by their names.

On the sensual side I found "Summer Song," "One

Enchanted Evening," "Sleepy Hollow" (though probably not the one where everyone gets their heads cut off), and "Starlight Express."

For mystery, there was "River Nile," "Shades of Gray," "Prairie Smoke," and "London Dawn."

Because it would inevitably turn out to be important to my wife's lawyer, I checked. In utter defiance of the odds, there was no "Pierce Brosnan's Eyes."

When did psycho-therapy take over the paint business? You can't just buy a can of paint anymore. You have to have an out-of-body experience.

More disturbing is that somewhere there are people thinking up names for these colors. Special people. People who can see colors normal people can't, in the same way dogs can hear sounds undetectable to the human ear.

Actually, it's probably a bunch of women. All of the color names for gray were pleasant and reassuring and vaguely boring. "Silver Hills," "Garden Home," and "White Knight."

If it was a man, gray would have names like "Daytona Exhaust," "Early Morning Tool Box," or "Smith & Wesson Surprise."

Meanwhile, a regular guy would come up with stuff like "Confederate Dead," "Hitler's Brain," and "Grandpa's Tongue."

I found one that seemed OK. By placing a color chit next to what's left of my libido after 25 years of marriage, I discovered that "Tornado" was both mysterious and sensual. Real tornados are scary and physical. Close enough.

Things got worse. Turned out that the store didn't actually carry "Tornado." What they have are a million cans of white paint, and a gatling gun color machine. You buy the paint and they mix the color you want.

The idea here is that all colors are just a combination of other colors. By adding the right amount of various, inert pigments, you get visions like "Baby's Smile," "Angel Song," and "Easter Bunny Vomit."

It took three people and five tries before they got it right. I was perfectly happy with the first result, which looked more like "Monsoon Mud," but Emily, Jill and Clint ganged up on me.

"Yuck," they said. "Let's try again."

Attempt # 2 looked more like a cheap imitation of "Wet Rat," while #3 tried hard to be "Drunk Tank Floor." #4 was somewhere in the neighborhood of "Horse Tranquilizer." The last one would have scared the hell out of Timothy Leary.

Out of ideas, Emily dabbed a bit of actual "Tornado" on a paint stick, and ran it through a computer. "Tornado" turned out to be a very genderless B-15.5, F-.5, L-1y47.

I took the paint home, where we got into a big fight over the really important issue of applying it with or against the wood grain.

Boy
of
Summer

In the summer of 1965, I played right field
for the Park Lane Lions. Talent had nothing to do with it.
Short one player to field a team, the Lions were desperate
enough to take even me.

I couldn't bat, field, run or even spit right. I succeeded
only in proving that I wasn't fit for baseball. Any effort I put
into the game constituted a minor form of suicide

It wasn't my fault. Baseball is a team sport. For people
like me, organized behavior is the first step toward involun-
tary servitude, which itself is only a wink away from outright
slavery.

The problem was that I couldn't pay attention. Standing a
mile away from the action, lugging a mitt constructed from
the hide of an entire cow, my mind constantly wandered to
buried treasure, space travel and kissing girls.

I was thus engrossed one lazy afternoon when a fly ball
came my way. I hadn't even been aware that anyone was at
bat. But since the crowd in the stands was screaming and
pointing in my direction, there had to be a ball on the way.

I ran about in an effort to locate the ball. When I couldn't find it in the sky, I ran to get out of its way. I ran completely off the field and into the parking lot. It was a huge waste of effort.

The crowd, which had monitored my frantic scuttling with growing concern, cheered when the ball finally reentered the earth's atmosphere and struck me squarely in the forehead.

It was my last baseball game. The huge purple lump on my head eventually went away, but not my antipathy toward the game.

Apparently, I still can't get out of the way. On Friday, friends Ann and Ken invited us to a Salt Lake Stingers game at Franklin Highly Effective Field. Another couple, Penrod and Cheryl, came along so they would have someone to talk baseball to. Good idea. Baseball is mostly talk, both on the field and in the stands. There are long periods when nothing is happening but the selling of expensive hot dogs.

In Little League, the talk centered mainly around the Big Leagues. The statistics of Drysdayle, Kofax, Mays and Mantle were rabidly debated by boys whose sole reason for existence was to be just like them.

Who had good stats? Where was the sweet spot? Should a runner slide feet or head first? Curves, sliders, heat, spit balls, and could Hank Aaron have beat up Babe Ruth? It's why they call baseball the thinking man's game.

On Friday, the Fresno Grizzlies were playing the Stingers. I'll spare you the suspense. They beat us 3-2. It soon became apparent to Ken and Penrod that I wasn't a worshipper of baseball. The main clue was that I didn't bring a mitt to catch foul balls whacked into the stands. I brought a helmet.

Listening to Ken and Penrod, I realized that baseball is still very much the thinking man's sport. Disturbingly so.

According to Ken, successful hitters of homeruns derive their success from having large behinds. Real sluggers, like fertile mothers, need a good set of hips to deliver. McGuire, Sosa, John Boy Walton's mom, they all have ample butts.

I'm guessing this is new baseball technology. It certainly never came up in Little League, and probably would have resulted in being chased home by your teammates if it had.

There were some interesting things at the game, even for non-fans such as myself. Local radio disc jockeys came out onto the field and used a compressed air cannon in the shape of an Oscar Meyer wiener to shoot wadded-up t-shirts into the stands.

Later, Frank Layden sang "Take Me Out To the Ballgame" so loud that large animals over at Hogle Zoo immediately went into estrus.

It was a great summer night and I'm glad I went. Baseball is definitely the thinking man's game, one we can all learn something from. I'm thinking I have got to get me one of those wiener guns.

A Dog to its Vomit

Thirty years ago, my friends and I walked out of Skyline High School. We swore a blood oath that we would never go back. As I recall, we sacrificed a chicken and everything.

I really owe that chicken an apology. On Saturday, about 400 members of the Skyline Class of 1971 gathered at Snowbird to see who got fat, bald, rich, divorced, augmented, etc. . . .

More than 900 of us departed Skyline, some by the skin of our teeth, others by the napes of their necks. Holding a reunion 30 years hence was the furthest thing from our oblivious minds.

On Saturday night, my first thought was that we did this reunion in the nick of time. Bell-bottom pants, acne and headbands had given way to dress slacks, wrinkles and hair-pieces. Any later and some of us would have shown up in bibs. There were characters and scenes straight out of *Romy and Michele's High School Reunion*. Personality is not one of the things guaranteed to improve with age. That's good. Aberrant behavior was the only thing still recognizable in some of us.

I wandered around trying to find familiar faces through the gray hair and pounds, getting the same blank looks I knew I was giving. (Maybe I went to school with you, or maybe I've just seen your face on the wall at the post office). Fortunately, someone had the forethought to put our yearbook pictures on our nametags. Then you could tell that the plump insurance rep in front of you was once the skinny guy who rode his motorcycle naked through a pep rally.

My own yearbook picture is horrible. It's not exactly a face you might see over the top of a banjo in Georgia, but certainly not the face of someone who was one day going to . . . what?

I had no idea what I was going to do after high school. Those of us who thought we did certainly had a few surprises coming.

On Saturday night, they handed out awards for some of these surprises, awards for the most kids, least hair, most divorces and fewest wrinkles.

There could have been a few more awards, trophies for biggest waistline, smallest paycheck, most arrests and shortest employment record. I could have gone home with the one for the most beatings.

None of this was stuff we planned to accomplish back when things were groovy, way back when being the teacher's pet was not necessarily synonymous with the teacher going to prison for 15 years.

The closest thing I had to a goal when I got out of high school was inventing a new drug, something that didn't annoy the cops and my mom. A few years later I *was* a cop. Now I drop Zantac.

Similar things happened to my friends, none of whom showed up for the reunion. They probably knew just how

71

ridiculous it is to drive down memory lane in anything but an armored car.

Bruce, who seemed immortal in '71, died in 1990. Bammer wanted to spend life wasted on a beach in California, but ended up an LDS bishop. Rusty, who our moms constantly nagged us to line up with our sisters, is gay. Boone advocated total revolution back then, but somewhere along the way decided to try his hand at being a CEO. Gidget, a guy everyone knew belonged in Special Ed, is a lawyer now.

Some things hadn't really changed. Thirty years after the night we graduated, I think the same number of people got drunk.

And me. The idiot who swore he was forever through with desks and deadlines still spends most of his time with them. Hell, newspaper work is like I never got out of Detention.

Ride 'em, Kirby!

Among the many things our venerated pioneer ancestors did was ride big, irritable animals. I mentioned this in the column on the Days of '47 Parade, prompting G.W. of West Jordan, to write:

"The horses in the parade are beautiful animals. Why did you have to write about them going to the bathroom?"

I apologize. Apparently, more explanation about horses was needed. That I failed to do this stems from little experience (and large fear) of animals big enough to knock me down and have their way with me. That's why I already was at work on a large animal column.

On Monday, I attended the Spanish Fork Fiesta Days Rodeo. For those who have never been, a rodeo is an event where people deliberately give giant animals every reason and opportunity to knock them down. Saner people pay money to watch.

Thousands of years ago, our ancestors walked everywhere. Then some lunatic whose name is lost to history (probably Brad, or Rowdy, or Buck), seized upon the idea of getting a horse to do the walking.

The horse first had to be convinced. My guess is that someone probably jumped on one. An argument ensued, during which the horse beat every lick of sense out of Brad, Rowdy, Buck and all their friends and neighbors.

Centuries later, the descendants of this ancient people are still trying to come to some sort of arrangement with the horse. The modern word "rodeo" actually descends from the prehistoric phrase, "Somebody go find the rest of Brad's pelvis."

Enough history. I just wanted to point out how rodeos came to be the loud, heavily promoted and thoroughly expensive events they are today.

If rodeo logic is a mystery, the method is marvelously simple. Basically, a human climbs on the back of a horse and tries to stay there for eight seconds. This is longer than it sounds. When a horse is mad at you, eight seconds can last up to four months.

It's also way harder than it sounds. For one thing, the rider can only use one hand. For another, huge bulls sometimes stand in for the horses. It's the difference between being thrown into the stands and being thrown into the parking lot.

Probably because it's more dangerous, bull riding is considered king of rodeo events. It's also the one event completely lacking any semblance of legitimate ranch work. Look, it's one thing to want to tame a horse to ride or hitch to a wagon, and another to climb on a bull because it's Saturday night and you're too drunk to know better.

There are other events, including calf roping and steer wrestling. I don't have room here to describe them, but picture what it would take to put pajamas on a 600 pound, four-year-old kid.

Speaking of kids, my favorite event of the evening was

the one called "Mutton Bustin'." In this event, young kids
were encouraged to ride sheep, an animal that many scientists
argue escapes being classified as a vegetable only by the
presence of hair.

No matter how tight a kid held on, eventually he ended up
slipping around and hugging the sheep's belly. According to
veteran animal riders, this is the most difficult riding trick to
master because it puts the rider between the ground and the
animal.

The kids were tough. They held on until the sheep gave
up and fell over asleep, or the riders got tired of plowing
furrows with their heads.

Mutton Bustin' looked like what you would get if the
Wizard of Oz had invented the Pony Express.

All in all, I liked the rodeo. It made more sense than
politics, took less time than church, and wasn't as dangerous
as a commute to Salt Lake.

Deliverance Lite

Tomorrow is the big, annual guy trip. Boone, Rusty, Gidget and I are leaving on a kayak trip in the Pacific Northwest to prove that we are real men, possibly even real stupid men.

We call this annual trek our Medicine Vision Testosterone Quest, or guy trip for short. Our significant others call it the annual Moron Migration, and even wager on our injury rate.

The guy trip replaced deer hunting about 15 years ago, when collective marriage counseling determined that we could no longer store dead animals in the garage for months at a time.

We do kinder man stuff now. We run rivers, climb mountains, drive long distances, and in general pretend that we are not paunchy, nearsighted men with jobs and mortgages. We didn't invent the guy trip. Ancient man once ventured into the unknown to test himself, have visions, and/or kill other men doing the same thing. He traveled light and he traveled fast.

The guy trip remains just as important today. Men have to get away from the office to find out who we really are, a process of discovery that sometimes requires the forensic examination of our dental work.

Ancient or modern, a guy trip is a highly ritualized event. At my house, the main ritual involves my wife searching my gear before I leave.

Being both a wife and a Canadian, Irene has a Mayberry P.D. approach to self-defense. I can take either a gun or bullets, not both.

When I holler about bears and sharks and forest monsters, she gives me a look that speaks volumes, this particular one titled, "Remember When You Shot Boone's Wetsuit Because You Thought It Was Bigfoot?"

Packing for a guy trip used to be easier. When I was a Scout, for example, the only required items for a successful guy trip were a hammer, Oreos, matches and assorted, salacious magazines. Dynamite was good, but harder to come by. Anyone who brought a flashlight, bug repellent, water, directions or even underpants was a momma's boy.

Hell, worrying our moms was the entire point of a guy trip. A Medicine Vision Testosterone Quest that didn't end in extended convalescence was considered a complete waste of time and insurance.

Ironically, it was just this attitude that eventually made packing for guy trips much more complicated. Gidget called an hour before the flight and asked if I had any room in my carry-on bag for his special, padded kayak seat.

Gidget's prostate has never recovered from being hammered flat on the 1996 bike trip we took over every logging road in the western U.S. He needs padding to sit down longer than five minutes.

I told him to get lost. I have my own special needs, one of which is an air mattress. Thanks to the great Sky Trip

Parachute Jump of 1978, my bones don't get a good night's sleep on bare ground anymore.

The paper sack that once carried everything I needed to survive a week-long trip into the wilds has been replaced by several nylon duffle bags containing gear necessary to just keep me at the level where I'll *want* to survive.

Allergy medication, Pepto-Bismol, Tylenol, proper food, pillow, socks, toilet paper, spare glasses, bear repellent, lantern, cell phone, shovel, laptop computer, emergency cash, rain gear, toothbrush and a snakebite kit. Oh, and lots of underwear.

These are a few of the things modern man needs to keep him lucid enough to have a good time while roughing it the way ancient man once did.

I don't care how ancient man did it way back when. Today's ancient man has more sense.

Kirby Does the Colorado

MOAB, UTAH—One hundred and thirty years ago, Major John Wesley Powell became the first person to successfully navigate the Colorado River without first obtaining a permit from the Bureau of Land Management.

To celebrate this achievement, I decided to follow in his footsteps as much as possible, while at the same time maintaining my physical and mental health. We ran the Colorado River from Moab to Hite.

Lacking the two main essentials for river running—a boat and common sense—we sought the services of a reliable rafting company. North American River Expeditions was chosen because of their reputation for fearless outdoor professionalism. Also, I found their card in a magazine.

When I called and explained my plans for a comprehensive documentary on river running, manager Dave Bodner said "We can do that."

Then I asked what the odds were of encountering giant squid or U-boats on the Colorado River. Dave said, "Are you that guy from the *Tribune*?"

Even so, North American set everything up. All we had to

do was follow their instructions.

And pay them, of course.

Probably to minimize the burden constituted by people showing up completely helpless (if not half naked and drunk), they sent us an equipment checklist and directions to Moab.

The equipment list included essential stuff like clothing, tent, flashlight, sunscreen, and optional stuff like camera and film, diary, alcoholic beverages, binoculars and reading material.

Take everything on the list, even if it sounds idiotic. By this I mean especially the rain gear. It may seem crazy to pack rain stuff for a trip into one of the most arid places in the country, especially since you plan on getting wet in the only water you encounter there, but do it anyway. We ran into a rainstorm on the second day that lasted an hour and was so heavy that it pounded the tops of our heads flat.

For good measure, we added to the list more sunscreen, mosquito netting, trade goods and a large elephant gun. Seriously, guns are not allowed on the trip. Tourists are dangerous enough without them.

§ § §

To get to Moab from Salt Lake City, just drive south until you get to a place that looks like God had a *really* good time making it. That's Moab. Stop driving and locate the office of your river outfitter. Because the town is small, this may seem like an easy thing to do. It is if you don't ask for directions.

During the summer, a large percentage of Moab's population has no idea what the hell is going on, and wouldn't be able to tell you if they did. They are not from around these parts, and they don't speak English.

Ask a stranger on a Moab street where something is, and nine times out of ten you will get, "Vo ist die Disneyland, bitte?" in return. Ignore them and continue your search.

Once the company is located, all that remains is to stow your gear aboard one of three different types of watercraft: a raft you paddle yourself, a raft you help paddle and a motorized pontoon. Keep in mind that space aboard all three is at a premium. Leave your television home.

One final item was needed—a river guide. When rafting white water for the first time, it's wise to bring along someone who knows what they are doing. Rapids have a nasty habit of lurking around corners. Worse, there is no reverse gear on a rubber raft. By the time you see a giant, sucking whirlpool filled with rabid Utah chub, it's too late.

Our guide from North American was Christian Dean, a 25-year-old, sun hammered, buccaneer-in-a-former-life river rat. When it came to river running, not only could Chris walk the walk, he talked the talk. His speech was a patois of stuff like "avast," "flogging," "yard arm" and "Get back in the #&%$! boat!" It was all very nautical.

The other member of the crew was the boat's swamper, Stacy Merz, a highly attractive, 24-year-old midwesterner, who "always wanted to be a river guide," even though it meant having to wait on a bunch of tourists. "Swamper" is just a nice river way of saying drudge.

The night before shoving off, we met up at the Gonzo Inn with the rest of the group, all of whom turned out to be foreigners. There was the McCord family from Boston, and a thirty-something couple from California. Chris and Stacey came by and answered our final questions.

First time voyagers have many nervous queries, most of

which center around personal issues such as personal safety and personal hygiene. Specifically, "Will we get killed?" and "Will there be a private place to go to the bathroom?" The answer to both is "Maybe."

I'm not trying to scare you, but think about it. People go white water rafting for the thrill. No risk, no thrill. They make you fill out an acknowledgement-of-risk form and everything. But if you pay attention and do exactly what the guide says, you will live long enough to need to go to the bathroom. Frankly, this is the part where you may wish that you got killed.

There are no bathrooms on the Colorado River. This highly personal need is handled by something ominously called "the groover." Worse, there are some places on the river where it's not always possible to completely conceal the act of "grooving."

Although the term refers to any of a number of portable chemical toilets, "the groover" originated from the early river running practice of doing one's business in a 20-millimeter ammo can, the edges of which are rather thin and sharp. Someone deduced a way of putting a toilet seat on the can, probably after someone else got sliced into thirds while going to the bathroom. The can was eventually replaced by a modern chemical toilet. Privacy, however, remains hard to come by on the river.

§ § §

The following morning, we drove 12 miles south of Moab to the Potash boat ramp where we put in. Our boat was a World War II-era pontoon, powered by a Mercury outboard which produced about the same amount of speed you might expect to get from a very tired duck.

Going slow is OK because there is a lot to see on the river. Besides, eventually the water goes a whole lot faster on its own than you really want it to.

A brief note about the water: because of a high silt content, the Colorado River looks a lot like Ovaltine. At some points, it stops just short of being mud.

Like John Wesley Powell, I kept a journal during part of our travels. Unlike every other documentary about the Colorado River, I shall quote from mine rather than his.

"Day One, 8:45 a.m. — Successfully launched our estimable craft at the Potash Marina. Weather fine, with notable exception of sun being hot enough to fry ham on our foreheads. Supplies holding out. River calm and highly brown in color. Vegetation consists of two or three indigenous weeds and 5 million linear miles of tamarisk, a tree so ugly that originally it must have been grown on Mars. No sign of local inhabitants. Vigilance is our watchword.

"8:58 a.m. — Encountering frequent clumps of a Cappuccino-like river foam, which our guide calls 'Indian soap.' Judging from the taste, it's really a natural froth whipped up by the current from plant oils leeched into the water. Violent retching.

"9:09 a.m. — Numerous tall cliffs. Lots of brown water. Many tamarisks.

"9:44 a.m. — Cliffs. Water. More #%*@! tamarisks.

"10:11 a.m. — No sign of sharks or enemy frogmen.

"10:31 a.m. — Spirits high despite captain's refusal to trade some of the women for a supply of rum.

"10:47 a.m. — [deleted mutinous observations]

"11:15 a.m. — This journal bites."

Tamarisk was introduced from Europe to California in 1901 as a method of controlling erosion. This giant weed soon made it's way up the Colorado corridor, choking out the native vegetation. It provides sullen shade mainly for voracious mosquitoes. Even beaver won't gnaw on it.

We didn't know this before, of course. Chris was a veritable encyclopedia of river lore, including the actual location where, during the filming of *Thelma & Louise*, a car was launched from the cliff tops. The first car was supposed to land in the river, but instead flew all the way across and bashed into the other side of the canyon because someone had the catapult turned up really high. A subsequent car landed in the river and was fished out and hauled away by helicopter.

§ § §

Although it's called "running" the Colorado River, there are opportunities for some optional walking. We stopped several times for short hikes to see local flora and fauna, including, once, a tarantula the size of a dust mop. Side canyons abound in petroglyphs and pictographs, petrified logs and Anasazi ruins.

Most of the ruins were Anasazi granaries or storage places for food. Hundreds of these dot the cliffs and ledges. Little is known of the Anasazis, who mysteriously vanished several hundred years ago. One theory (my own actually) is that they were the first political party of Strom Thurmond. Their cliff writings are unclear on this, however. The boat crew opined that the squiggles and lines etched into one cliff told stories of memorable harvests and hunts. However, as the boat's resident scribe, I was able to deduce that the ancient communique more clearly stated "Two Gopher Heads loves Pretty Woman Belcher."

We camped that night on a sand bar wider, but slightly shorter than Kentucky. While we took our leisure setting up tents and beating mosquitoes senseless, Chris and Stacey made camp and cooked. In fact, they did just about all of the work. It was like having your very own slaves, or it was until they got annoyed and threatened me with a boat hook. At any rate, the food was terrific.

Later, when the sun went down, I sprawled on the sand and watched bats and satellites and the Milky Way. I felt sorry for the people in passing airliners, on their way to boring places like the French Riviera and Tahiti.

At dawn, we headed for the much anticipated Cataract Canyon. We stopped briefly near the confluence of the Green and Colorado Rivers, to register for a campsite (provided that we lived to see it) on the other side of the rapids.

For people who hadn't been paying attention along the way, a big sign here announces, "Danger! The Surgeon General has determined that river running can be even worse for your health than smoking, especially if you drown." Or words to that effect.

Before heading into the rapids, we donned life preservers, cinching them up until our faces turned purple. Then we received a pep talk from the boat crew. Instructions mainly consisted of what to do if you fell out of the boat in the middle of the rapids: essentially nothing. The river would have its way with you no matter what you did. The boat would meet you somewhere downstream, possibly Baja California.

Although the water is low in late summer, an experienced boat captain knows how to make the best of what there is. Plunging into the rapids, Chris handled the boat masterfully, performing many dexterous maneuvers he later confided were called "Hose the Reporter."

This turned out to be considerably less amusing than it sounds. Water with a high content of silt is not the sort of water you want up your nose. Mainly because it later returns to the light of day as adobe, an astonishingly durable form of Native American spackle. The following morning I sneezed and shot a hole through a tree.

The rapids in Cataract Canyon have colorful names that reflect historical events or sheer human awe of natural forces at work. There was a vicious stretch of water called Satan's Gut, and another known as Powell's Pocket Watch, so named because Powell allegedly lost his time piece here. Also Little Niagara, Capsize, Red Wall, Big Drop 3, Mile Long, Bladder-Voiding Gulch, and a personal favorite, Nine Hysterical Tourists.

As if that wasn't enough fun, it started to rain as we came out of the rapids and into the upper reaches of Lake Powell. The drizzle only lasted for a few minutes. Then it started to pour, progressing almost immediately into something best described as a beating. The water came down in such volume that we might as well have been riding underneath the pontoon.

Oddly enough, this produced the best Kodak moment. Hundreds of small waterfalls soon spilled from the cliff tops. Only one posed a problem, growing in size until it began shooting boulders, logs and Japanese tourists clear out into the main channel.

§ § §

We camped that night at Sheep Canyon. The following day, we drifted on down to Hite, stopping briefly for one last opportunity to hurt ourselves by jumping off cliffs into the water.

Cliff jumping is much harder than it sounds, mainly because water does not compress well. Jumping into water from a height of 30 feet is about the same as landing on damp concrete. Worse, the water goes places it normally shouldn't. And if your swimming suit is in the way, it will get taken along for the ride as well.

Three days and 100 miles after leaving Moab, we arrived at Hite, which has all the ear-markings of a thriving resort community in the Gobi Desert. Seriously, there isn't much at Hite except a place to fall out of the boat and crawl to your car.

Following in the footsteps of Powell turned out to be more colorful and enjoyable than we'd thought. Except for the sunburns, we would definitely do it again.

A Grandpa is Born

I became a grandfather at 11:47 a.m. on Saturday. Her name is Hallie Tribune Morgan. Tribby for short.

OK, that was almost true. After a huge family fight, Hallie's real middle name ended up being Elizabeth. Tribby for short.

Everything else went fine. I can say that because I stood out in the hall where I belonged during the scary, painful part. Having been three times a father and eleven years a cop, I find absolutely nothing endearing or beautiful about the miracle of life.

The fun part doesn't start until the kid is cut, wrapped and delivered.

No, a grandfather's job on the big day is to stand around and make sure everyone at the hospital looks like they know what they are doing. This is way harder than it sounds. For starters, nobody at a hospital looks a particular part anymore. When I saw another guy my age helping a very pregnant young woman into a wheelchair, I made the mistake of asking him if he was going to be a grandfather too.

"It's my first CHILD, thank you very much," he said.

The medical staff at St. Mark's was equally deceiving. Housekeepers look like nurses, nurses look like doctors, and doctors . . . well, our doctor was a blond woman.

Times have changed since Hallie's mom was delivered by Marcus Welby, M.D. On Saturday, Dr. Elizabeth (no relation to the birthed) Bergquist came running up the hall and started giving orders.

Actually, she only gave one. She pointed at me, and said to the staff, "That man is a newspaper columnist. Do not let him near any drugs, fire alarms or babies."

When she said that, all the nurses jumped up and shouted, "Stat!"

I checked. "Stat" is medical jargon for "We must bill these people a lot of money in a hurry."

The "hurry" part was OK with us because, quite obviously, the time was getting close. Grandparents instinctively know these things. Also, noises had started coming out of Christie's room that sounded like someone was neutering a fully conscious panther.

When the noises reached demonic levels, medical personnel raced into the room, slammed the door, and got busy paying off their student loans.

Even so, it took another six days for us to become grand-parents. It seemed that long. For some reason, everything at a hospital is in a big hurry that still ends up taking forever. Maybe it's anticipation. Something about having your ear pressed against a door causes time to slow and stretch until something as simple and natural as having a baby takes about as long as a congressional audit.

No problem. The waiting gave me ample opportunity to think about how all our lives were going to change from this first birth.

Scott was going to become a father. Christie's sisters would finally be aunts. My parents would be great-grandparents. We would have to get a restraining order for Larry Erdmann.

The role I was destined for would be a major one. As the patriarch of my growing clan, people would look to me for strength and wisdom. I would have to say wise things.

My wife saw me pacing the hall and left her vigil near the keyhole of the delivery room to calm me down. She knew I was struggling with the way things were going to be now.

Her: "This is so exciting. Are you ready to be a grandfather?"

Me: "Yeah, but I'm still a little squirmy about sleeping with a grandma."

Much later, someone came out to a parking lot across the street and told me that everything had gone well.

Run, Bambi, Run!

With just three days left to the opening of the deer hunt, we should probably cover some important safety tips.

If this is your first hunt, please remember to shoot responsibly at stuff that may be closer to China than it is to you. Technically, deer are brown. Hunters, orange.

If you've been hunting deer for years, today is the final deadline for laying off the Hostess products. Even among hunters, it's embarrassing to have a stroke 20 feet from where you parked the truck.

For deer, Saturday would be an excellent time to begin a two-week moratorium on all outdoor activities.

Perhaps the most important safety tip is to keep your head down if you plan on hunting anywhere in the North-Eastern Unit. My friends and I are thinking about trying our luck out near Vernal.

Don't worry about us shooting your buck. We have not noticeably hit a deer since 1988, when Gidget threw a rock at one he caught eating his trail mix.

Our lack of success is due in part to the fact that we are

all phenomenally horrible hunters. We're noisy, argumentative, lazy and utterly directionless. True story: one year, we got completely lost setting up a tent.

Stuff like this should take all the fun out of hunting deer. Not the stupid ones that jump in front of cars, of course. I mean the smart ones, the ones that know how to become invisible.

But we're actually looking forward to the hunt this year. Our goal is to bag a poacher. Boone got his first last year, and hasn't shut up about it since. Claims he took him down with a cell phone at 300 yards.

It happened like this: while hunting out near Strawberry, Boone and Rusty saw some idiot shoot a cow elk. They immediately called the poaching hotline on a cell phone, and gave them the guy's description and vehicle license number.

The "immediately" part is actually a bit of a stretch. They had to hike back to camp for the hotline number in a copy of the Big Game Proclamation. After a brief fight over who used it to start last night's fire, they borrowed another copy from the next camp.

Anyway, the guy got arrested and convicted.

Boone isn't the only one stalking poachers. According to the wildlife cops I've talked to, calls to the poaching hotline during this year's elk hunt rival the number of calls received during all hunts last year.

While an increase in the number of cell phones in the field is responsible for some of this, I'd also like to think that responsible hunters are fed up with taking the rap for bad ones.

So, if you plan on bagging a poacher this year, we should probably go over a few important tips to consider when hunting by cell phone.

First, you might want to know the number. Not having it handy compares to leaving the ammo for your rifle at home. The number is 1-800-662-DEER, or, for people who hate that sort of thing, 1-800-662-3337.

You'll hear a recording when you call. Wait, and then press 1. Your call will be forwarded to an actual wildlife cop, whose first responsibility might be to talk you out of shooting the poacher.

Taking a poacher follows similar rules to taking a deer. You need basic stuff like age, sex, direction of travel, etc. . . . Even better are details like license number, vehicle description, fingerprints and credit card expiration date.

The more information you have, the more likely you are to get your poacher. Best of all, there's no limit, restricted areas or once-in-a-lifetime tags on this kind of a hunt. Poachers are always in season.

Happy hunting.

Mountain Mouse Massacre

No deer hunt ever goes entirely according to plan. This is what I'm thinking at 6:42 a.m. Saturday, while simultaneously toying with the idea of shooting Ralph.

Fortunately for Ralph, I have no bullets and no idea where we are. It's dark, freezing, and we're going 100 mph through large stands of scrub oak and cows, on our way to his extra secret deer hunting spot.

According to Ralph, the odds of filling our tags at his secret spot were excellent. Deer had been seen in the area as recently as 1968.

If you're interested, Ralph's extra secret hunting spot is somewhere on top of Billies Mountain. As near as I can tell, it's about 15 miles due south of Provo as the crow flies, or twice around North Africa as Ralph drives.

I feel comfortable revealing the location of Ralph's extra secret hunting spot, mainly because it turned out to be surrounded by "No Trespassing" signs. It's so secret, even the deer don't know where it is.

If the secret hunting spot had ever been an actual secret, it wasn't anymore. When we pulled off the highway to unload the ATVs, there was more traffic than a Kenny Rogers concert. Ralph said not to worry.

We got to Ralph's secret spot shortly before daybreak. Veteran hunters know that this is the perfect time to be in place. Deer start to move at first light, which is precisely when everyone starts shooting. Being in place significantly reduces your odds of being mistaken for a deer.

Here things began to go bad. First light of opening day normally sounds like the Tet Offensive. Indeed, there are some parts of Utah where the sound of early morning gunfire directed at deer can actually be heard on the moon.

This time it was silent. The sun came up and nobody shot. Nobody did anything. Nobody was there. Rocketing along in the dark, we had driven into the middle of a posted area roughly the size of Somalia.

It would have been worse if there *had* been any deer. In an effort to make it worse, we went looking for some. With Ralph leading the way, this involved riding our ATVs the long way around to New Mexico. When we got there, we found some deer. They were all unshootable doe.

A general rule of deer hunting is that if you haven't killed anything by noon of opening day, chances are pretty good that you won't. So we were relieved when, shortly before noon, our luck changed.

At precisely 11:38 a.m., Ralph ran over a mouse.

Since we were hunting for meat, we kept it. On the way back down to the trucks, I figured the cost ratio of the meat, factoring in time, gas, injuries, license fees and general aggravation. Cut and wrapped, the mouse came to about $8,900 per pound. More if we had picked up Hanta virus from handling it.

Things couldn't possibly get any worse, I thought. Unfortunately, thinking this way while on a deer hunt constitutes having an actual plan. And things never go according to plan.

Driving down the mountain, I bashed in the front of my truck when I swerved to miss a two point buck and hit an embankment, a large ditch and a tree.

Limping home, I realized that this year's hunt was still better in terms of cost to life and limb than the deer hunt of '72, when Bammer and I accidentally burned down his dad's trailer. Maybe the deer hunt hadn't gotten weirder. Maybe I was just out of practice.

Even though all I had to show them was the mouse, I pulled into a game checking station in Spanish Fork Canyon. The game wardens weren't interested. They were collecting brains. They had a big box of them.

"If you tagged anything, we need to check the brain for disease," one of the wardens said. "We'll just lop the top of the skull off and lift it out."

I knew he was talking about deer brains. But after riding all over creation with Ralph, I knew of only one diseased brain for sure. I seriously considered taking off my hat.

Emptied Nest

My daughter moved out last week.
She relocated to Moab, a highly scenic and strangely inhabited part of the state.

Before Autumn left, her mother and I gave her (in addition to a large wad of money) our best advice.

Mom: "Please make sure to wear your seat belt, save your money, keep your doors locked, drink plenty of milk, take your vitamins, and call us every single night without fail."

Me: "Do not date any Germans."

Periodically, Moab is the scene of many Germans. While I have nothing against them other than I can't understand a word they say outside of "BMW," I don't want my daughter marrying one and moving even farther away.

It's a big deal when kids move out. Suddenly there's all this space to put a pool table that, for some reason beyond male comprehension, gets turned into a sewing room instead.

If you don't count all the times she ran away, the two times she was abducted by aliens, and four previous trial runs at living on her own, this is Autumn's first time away from home.

My own experience leaving home was much shorter in duration. As I recall, my dad said to me, "The police are here."

Anyway, I'm something of an expert on children leaving home.

Psychologists refer to this behavior in kids as "leaving the nest." It's a developmental phase in everyone's life immediately preceded by a parental phase known as "Go get your own damn worms."

Not counting the one my parents used, children leaving home typically do so via four basic methods. Keep in mind that none of these involve loaning or selling them to a research company.

First, you can pay the treasure of your heart to move out. By this I do not mean that you blatantly offer your child a giant cash settlement. They might use it to get their belly button pierced.

I was thinking more of underwriting the first six months' rent for an apartment in North Korea. Tests have shown that the Far East is far enough away to keep your child from coming home every other day to eat and look for spare change.

In the second method, the child does not have to move. Home does. You simply get a realtor and sell the home out from under them. Hey, it's tough to move back in with Mom and Dad if you don't know where they are.

Third, the kid gets married. This may cause children to want to build a nest of their own, somewhere far enough away where Mom and Dad won't be able to give them tips on something called "the birds and the bees."

Finally, the child will move because he or she can no longer tolerate being asked to do heinous stuff like washing dishes or picking up their clothes. In my brother's and my case, it was to stop test firing high-powered rifle loads in our bedroom.

While independence is the most common reason for kids moving out, it's almost always followed by an intense period of disillusionment, when the child discovers that clean clothes do not appear by magic.

Parents, too, can suffer from the departure of children. For example, I hit my head on the ceiling fan jumping up and down for joy. Wait, I meant grief.

For some reason, it's tougher on women when children leave. They may experience something called the "empty nest syndrome." If your wife starts dressing the dog in baby clothes, you know she's got it bad.

While it's nice to have Autumn gone, we plan on visiting her a lot. Finding where she lives is easy. We just get in the car and follow our hearts.

Happy Ghoul's Day

Beginning around noon today, suburban yards will fill up with all sorts of weird, desperate creatures. Some will look funny, others strange, the rest simply demonic.

Do not be fooled. These are political candidates and/or campaign volunteers. The real trick-or-treaters don't officially start until about 3 p.m.

When I was a kid, trick-or-treating in broad daylight was a crime. If not an actual felony, it was at least a major social gaffe. No self-respecting kid went out while the sun was up. It was hard enough to get away with stuff at night.

For example, when he saw us cramming his cat into a mailbox one Halloween, old man Waddell hit Leon in the head with a caramel apple hurled from the porch.

It was enough that the pitch knocked Leon's plastic hillbilly teeth onto the neighbor's roof. Given sufficient light to see us better, Mr. Waddell would have also called our parents, possibly even the cops.

When someone did call the cops, we needed darkness to get away. Even the slowest cop can't miss the description of "a werewolf, a mummy and some kid wearing a plastic trash bag for a vampire cape."

No, real trick-or-treating can only be done at night. You can't lurk at high noon. This middle-of-the-day looting is just plain bad form. It defeats the very purpose of being a goblin. Speaking of which, there used to be a lot more monsters on Halloween. Blood and fangs are giving way to an increasing amount of cute. This is wrong. Any kid who went as a clown or an elf 35 years ago risked getting run out of the neighborhood.

Costumes cost a lot more than they once did. The last time I went trick-or-treating, my costume was an old sheet, a bunch of Band-Aids and a bottle of ketchup. Not counting getting grounded for using my mom's best linen, the whole thing cost less than three bucks.

Conversely, a professionally made railroad-crossing-accident-victim costume, if you can even find one these days, costs at least fifty bucks.

It's not the fault of kids. The entire Halloween industry has changed. Costumes must be flame-retardant, light reflective, waterproof, and have eyeholes in them big enough to stick your entire head through.

There were no plastic wounds, fake tattoos or protruding eyeball kits back then. We did it all ourselves with a Magic Marker. Halloween pirate tattoos didn't come off until Christmas.

I will concede that kids are much more politically correct these days. Once, Leon, Ronny and I put a great deal of effort into our ghost costumes. Even though it was the `60s, we were young enough to be stupid about certain racial issues.

Fortunately, the first house we hit was Ronny's. I thought his old man would die laughing. His mom had better sense though. She dragged us inside and fixed the pointy hoods on our ghost costumes.

Frankly, I wouldn't be writing this today if Ronny's uncle had opened the door and found three really short Klansmen on his porch.

My personal best costume was the year I went as a tombstone. I painted a cardboard box gray, wrote an epitaph on the front, and then cut a hole in the top for my head.

As costumes went, the tombstone showed a lot of imagination, but little sense. For one thing, it really restricted movement. I couldn't walk very fast or bend over. That was the Halloween that I spent two hours flat on my back in a ditch.

Halloween isn't what it used to be. When the kids start coming around this year, I'll have to show them the real spirit of trick-or-treating. I'm passing out political fliers instead of candy.

Something Winter This Way Comes

Even though snow has already fallen in parts of Utah, it's not too late to winterize. Doing so now may prevent costly repairs, legal fees, physical therapy and even cannibalism later on.

Winterizing refers to the process of preparing your home, vehicles and self for prolonged exposure to the cold. The word itself comes from the old English combination of the words "winter" and "terrorize."

The easiest (though hardly most sensible) way of winterizing is to drive to Mexico and remain there until May, or until you are extradited.

A cheaper way is to nail your doors and windows shut and watch TV for the same amount of time.

Unfortunately, neither of these options provides any protection for stuff that may be stuck outside during the winter: water pipes, pets, lawn furniture, the elderly and possibly your job.

According to prolonged yelling by my wife, responsible winterizing covers three basic areas: vegetable, animal and mineral.

Keep in mind that I am going by memory here. The last time I actually winterized was February. So, it's been a while. Also, there was a major water pipe explosion in April.

VEGETABLE—This part refers to getting the yard ready. Even though by design it's supposed to stay outside all year long, there are parts of a yard that cannot take the cold.

For some reason that makes sense only to a wife, leaves cannot take the cold. That's why it's important to gather them up and place them in trash bags for the winter, preferably before the first snow.

Depending on how many trees there are within leaf falling radius of your yard (14.5 miles), winterizing all the leaves in it could take as long as a Constitutional amendment.

There are a number of ways to gather leaves. Most people use rakes, blowers or vacuums. However, for long-term leaf winterizing, I've found that a chain saw works best.

There's also some other stuff here about covering roses, bringing potted plants inside, and tilling up the garden.

ANIMAL—Be sure to winterize all animals and children. This is particularly true if you plan on leaving them outside for any length of time, including basically forever.

Most animals are incapable of expressing to humans the fact that they are cold. That's why it's important to make sure they have a dry shelter, one that gives them protection from the wind. In some cases, a heat source may be necessary.

Kids, on the other hand, will always tell you when they want to come in from the cold. Sometimes by screaming, other times by setting the garage on fire.

Ironically, kids are also the animal with the least amount of common sense about the cold. If yaks are freezing solid outside, you still have to remind a kid to wear a coat.

MINERAL—In its original form, ice is a liquid. It doesn't become a mineral until prolonged exposure to something scientists call "driving conditions."

Ice has an adverse effect on a number of things that need to be winterized, including vehicles, driveways, sidewalks and water pipes.

Prolonged buildup of ice inside a car engine will prevent the car from starting. Heavy concentrations of ice on sidewalks may cause people to fall in a variety of amusing ways, something that can turn suddenly serious if it's your mother-in-law, or they know a lawyer.

Ice buildup inside water pipes is the worst. Allowed to go unchecked, it will make your house blow up in the spring. It won't be an actual explosion. More like the fire department is conducting some training in your attic.

Proper winterization here is to wrap pipes with protective foam, properly service your vehicle, and make sure you have a video camera handy when your mother-in-law comes to visit.

Giblet Tidbit Trivia

Thanksgiving is next week. If you are a holiday traditionalist, this gives you barely enough time to prepare for the big day.

The traditional family Thanksgiving feed is a highly complicated affair. Strict attention to detail results in a culinary masterpiece the entire family will enjoy, provided that it first doesn't start a brawl.

Tradition causes stress. More than a few people will end up in jail this Thanksgiving, thanks to a lunatic in a frilly apron and a June Cleaver hairdo, insisting that no one eat until the cranberry forks get polished.

So begin preparing for the big day now. This is particularly true when it comes to the business of turkey acquisition. It's not a traditional Thanksgiving feed without one.

Turkey as the centerpiece of the traditional Thanksgiving Day feast is a custom started by the Pilgrims, who, being from England, also ate a large number of eels.

Fortunately for us (and good taste), it was the turkey that captured America's heart and stomach. There's very little Norman Rockwell appeal in giving thanks over a platter of baked eel.

There are a number of ways to acquire a Thanksgiving Day turkey, several of which are highly illegal. In the interest of public safety (and personally, not getting sued), today's column will cover only the legal ones.

The obsessive traditionalist may wish to go out and get his or her own turkey from the wild. After all, that's how the Pilgrims did it.

Several days ago, I watched a turkey hunt on the "Guns, Gills and Guts" Channel. Two guys set out a bunch of attractive female turkey decoys, then used a turkey call to summon a male turkey.

Contrary to popular opinion, wild turkeys are very smart. It took hours of turkey calling (a noise that sounds a lot like choking Judge Judy) to lure a male turkey within range.

When he spotted the decoys, Tom Turkey casually slipped off his wedding ring before strutting on in. He was dropping hints about his annual income, when—BLAM!—he was food.

This, of course, is the way the Pilgrims got their Thanksgiving turkeys. Also, anything else they wanted to eat that had a mind of its own. Back then, shopping for food was a loud and bloody business.

You could raise your own turkey. It's not very hard. Unlike wild turkeys, most domestic turkeys have really small brains that they don't use except for finding ways to get killed long before Thanksgiving.

Also, be advised that turkeys raised in a back yard can be very tough, especially if they are allowed to form gangs. The two turkeys our neighbors had pecked most of the hair off their German shepherd.

The most common method of acquiring a turkey is to buy one at the store. The nice part here is that store turkeys are already dead. In fact, rigor mortis has set in to the extent that it will be days before you can eat it.

Thanks to an increasing number of boyfriends and son-in-laws at our table, we needed a big turkey for Thanksgiving. We found one just the right size. Frozen solid, it was like dragging a gun safe through the checkout line.

You should completely defrost a store turkey before cooking it. At room temperature, this process takes about the same amount of time as a presidential election. So please, use a welder.

I am, of course, just kidding. Even with a welder and a large magnifying glass, it takes days to make a store turkey feel like something other than a curling stone.

The important thing is to start now. There are just nine days until Thanksgiving, just barely enough time to give up and go buy a mess of eels.

Spending Christmas: Attention K-mas Shoppers

The day after Thanksgiving found me mingling with other eager shoppers at Target. Since 99 percent of the entire world was there, you and I probably saw/trampled each other.

Anticipating the traditionally huge bargains offered on this special day, shoppers began gathering outside stores shortly after midnight. They sipped hot chocolate, sang carols, and offered holiday greetings.

It was all a facade. The main reason for showing up eight hours before sunrise is to grab stuff before everyone else gets it.

Minutes before the doors opened, the crowd began creeping forward until the first line of shoppers looked like pressed ham against the glass. It was a middle-aged mosh pit.

When the doors finally opened, the pressure of the crowd was such that the first 20 shoppers were propelled toward the back of the store with enough force to cause them to warp into another dimension. Anyway, we never see them again.

What followed was a barely controlled riot. As the mob fanned out through the store for the bargains, small children were held aloft to prevent them from being crushed, or perhaps to offer them for sale.

After an hour of elbow throwing and another two hours standing in line, I had a facial tic so severe that it involved my glutes, and an uncontrollable desire to set fire to a series of orphanages.

At least by then I had my Christmas bargains: 300 feet of PVC pipe at 10 percent off, a case of imitation chocolate-covered imitation cherries and a Huckleberry Hound video.

I wanted a television, a *Gladiator* DVD and some white chocolate mints. Unfortunately, I couldn't bring myself to knock down other consumers fast enough to get there before they were snatched up and placed on layawaste by the first six shoppers.

I was lucky that I got something at all. Anything left on the shelves ten minutes after stores opened was a) technically on sale, and b) a bargain if you didn't have to bite someone else to make them let go of it.

Shopping the day after Thanksgiving was not the idea of virtually every guy I talked to Friday morning. We were all there because of the women in our lives, namely that we're afraid of them.

Bargain hunting, like marriage and menopause, is very much a female-dominated sport. It involves a process that guys cannot understand. If it did, we would soon stop kidding ourselves that hunting deer was a cost effective way of getting meat.

It's women that manage most family resources, and consequently it's women who bargain hunt. According to a fundamental, biological law, it works like this:

The basic woman inherently understands cost ratios, including the fuel it took to reach the store and the long-term effects any purchase will have on family finances. She will then buy whatever it is, including a truckload of beets, so long as is says "two for one" somewhere in the advertisement.

Meanwhile, guys think, "No way could I ever have too many ball-peen hammers."

Friday morning was very much a bargain moment. This is why most of the male shoppers had a vacant beast-of-burden expression. It did a poor job of masking our serious desire to be anywhere else, including work, combat, the moon or even church.

Woman: "OK, we got the VCR for Aunt Babette, the microwave for grandma, and the CD player for Lester. Now we just need a gun safe for your brother."

Guy: [Forlorn noise approximating the bray of a donkey].

Experts say that shoppers forked over an estimated $850 million to merchants on Friday. The fact that we gave it up with so little violence says that we are finally making some progress as a species. And that it's still early in the season.

Stringing Yule Along

It's time for another public service announcement, this one sponsored by some local attorneys. The idea being that it will drive some divorce, personal injury and estate management work their way.

Announcement: begin putting up your Christmas lights.

The attorneys also wanted me to suggest you do this in the middle of the night, dressed only in your underwear, while heavily intoxicated. No way. I'm still getting sued for that public service announcement about fireworks.

In the annals of really stupid human endeavors, few things surpass "Beverly Hills 90210," or nuclear warfare. But stringing colored lights on the roof of a house comes real close.

No one knows for sure why the tradition of Christmas lights began. The common theory is that they served as navigational aids for Santa. But since Santa was shot down over North Korea in 1951, this may not be true.

More believable is the claim that all those confusing lights are actually a spin-off from the glitzy and tasteless method used to let retired people know where Wayne Newton is singing.

It doesn't really matter. The thing to remember is that Christmas lights are the number one cause of holiday divorces, and the second leading cause of dashing through the snow with the cops after you.

To avoid these problems, please refer to this handy list of Christmas light dangers. I use it every year, and I'm still alive/married.

First, the best place to test Christmas lights is on the ground. Nothing is more frustrating than being forced by someone you love to go back up on a slippery roof because one light in 8,000 "is blinking a teensy bit out of sequence."

There are two basic methods to test the lights, both of which require an electrical outlet. While some people still believe that Christmas lights work by magic, the truth is that they mainly work by luck.

For example, you're extremely lucky if all the lights light when you plug them in. If an individual bulb doesn't light, try wiggling it. Sometimes it's just a short. The rest of the time the glass bulb will break off in your hand.

No matter how much sense it makes at the time, do not stick your finger or tongue into the open socket. That is where the electricity is. Contact with it will cause Christmas colored sparks to shoot out every one of your body's orifices, including the really small ones.

For replacement bulbs, go to a hardware or department store. You might even try an animal shelter or a real estate office. It doesn't matter, because the chances of finding the exact size bulb you need are the same at all of them.

If you do happen to locate the right size, rest assured that it will be the wrong color. This is bad. The same person who can't stand one light blinking out of sequence cannot tolerate two green bulbs next to each other.

Official Christmas light colors, as determined by the U.S. Department of Martha Stewart, are red, blue, green, orange and white. Pink works, but only if your house is also a brothel.

Attaching the lights to the roof can be tricky. Never use a nail gun, a welder or small children to hold the lights in place. Instead, buy a handy set of plastic clips that attach to the edge the roof.

The edge of a roof is no place for a fool, a drunk or an overweight, middle-aged man, unless you happen to be all three at the same time.

Finally, never string lights on a roof while receiving directions from someone on the ground. The two perspectives—perfection and survival—are not compatible.

Good luck. Merry Christmas. Happy holidays. Break a leg.

On Trax
for
X-mas

My family made the annual Christmas
pilgrimage to see the Temple Square lights Tuesday night.
We've done it every year since our kids were old enough to
sulk if we didn't.

Exactly why we make the trek depends on which side of
the family you ask. The kids and mom claim it's because of
tradition. From such experiences are valuable family memo-
ries born.

I say we're slow learners. It's a position I've maintained
since the Christmas of '82, or the highly memorable
"Christmas that the carriage horse blew slobber all over
Dad. Ha!"

It's exactly 44.2 miles from our house to Temple Square.
That's in a straight line, a direction of travel that only applies
to crows, light and artillery. Being humans, we have to drive
there by way of Peru.

This year was going to be different. This year we were
going to drive only half the distance (Panama), park the car,
and ride Trax downtown. The brilliant idea being that we
avoid a lot of aggravating traffic.

According to a UTA television commercial, Trax takes thousands of cars off the road every day. The only difference, they claim, is the serenity found in not having to drive or worry about downtown parking

I'm OK with that. It's certainly more legal than my favorite commuting dream of removing the same number of cars with a laser cannon, and much less expensive than building my own personal freeway.

However, I would like to point out something that UTA forgot to mention about riding Trax. Namely, that all the people in those thousands of other cars are now in the same car as you.

So, not only are those other people still in the way, you're close enough to notice that they have dandruff as well. It's perhaps a subtle difference.

Your personal Trax experience might be better. It certainly will be if you take it when the Jazz are not playing a home game. The only way it could have been more crowded Tuesday night is if UTA resorts to vacuum packing.

We got on the train at the Sandy Civic Center stop, or 10000 South. Just like subways in big cities, Trax stops have pleasant names like Fashion Place, Murray Central, Millcreek, Central Pointe and Ballpark.

Eventually, when Trax extends to points north and south, we will get other stops like Oil Refinery, Steel Mill, State Prison and Central Marsh.

Unlike big city mass transit, it's impossible to get lost on Trax. Mainly because ours only goes two places: the Delta Center and Sandy. If you miss your stop, stay on the train. Eventually you'll come back to it.

A primary difference in Trax vs. car is the level of politeness required. In your car, you can scream rude observations about the mental faculties of nearby commuters.

On Trax, it's a pretty good idea if you keep this stuff to yourself. Not only is it against the rules, you won't be able to get away from the offended party until the next stop.

It was interesting to see how people behaved when the cars got full. I'm pleased to announce that only once was a teenage boy dragged out of a seat so that a pregnant woman could sit down.

The rest of the time, teenagers were getting up so the elderly and disabled could sit down. Men got out of their seats so that women wouldn't have to stand.

Believe it or not, I actually saw some kid with purple hair spikes, chains and a nail through his nose, get up so that a mother with a baby could sit.

Maybe it takes riding this close to remind us that the milk of human kindness hasn't gone completely sour in our commute.

Being Kris Kringle

It is an unwritten Christmas law: the only thing tougher than waiting for Santa Claus is being Santa Claus.

Thanks to the management of the University Mall, I went undercover on Monday to examine this little known part of Christmas. If you were there between 6:30-7:30 p.m., the Santa you saw there was me. And if your kids no longer believe in Santa because of this, it's not my fault. I do a better Easter Bunny.

Guiding me through it all was Todd Bendall, ex-Marine, parent and 14-year Santa vet. It was Bendall's suit and accumulated wisdom that made this view from the other side of the beard possible.

"I believe in Santa Claus," Bendall said, helping me suit up by strapping an unnecessary pillow around my girth. "You will too once you see the eyes on these kids. When they see you, you'll start feeling like the real thing."

I wasn't so sure at first. For one thing, a Santa Claus suit traps 99.9% of your body heat and makes you feel like a woolly mammoth in drag. The beard and wig itch, and you can't see your feet for the pillow.

But Bendall was right. Encountering the first wide-eyed child in the mall, all my self-consciousness vanished as I bent down and said, "Ho-ho-ho."

The kid shrieked in horror and fled.

"Try sounding more jolly," Bendall suggested.

A few minutes later, I was sitting in a sled, facing a long line of rapture-fueled boys and girls, each and every one of them with a list of demands that would shame a Barbary Coast pirate.

According to Bendall, there are two rules that a Santa should never break: never promise a child anything and never say or do anything that would diminish their sense of self-worth. All of which proves that the real Santa is neither Democrat nor Republican.

Posing as Santa is an art form, an all-male one at that. Feminism has made few advancements into the arena of St. Nick, in part because it requires a baritone laugh and a bit of a paunch. But also because Santa is at heart a disciplinarian. Velvet suit and fur trim aside, Santa must maintain a slight aura of macho.

Kids are cool with this because of the timeless Santa tradition of bringing toys to good kids and lumps of coal to bad ones. Forget the Judgement Bar and destroying angels, kids know that the true test of a person's worth is found under the tree Christmas morning.

Being that it's still the Nineties, I took it upon myself to present a kinder and gentler Santa, one a bit more understanding on the whole naughty/nice issue. As such, I went for a realistic cross-examination of the kids who ventured onto my lap.

Me: "Have you been whacking your sister?"

Kid: "No."

Me: "Not even a little bit?"

Kid: "No."

Kid's sister: "Yes you have, Jeremy!"

Kid (mortified): "Wait..."

Me: "Hey, it's OK. She probably deserved it. Now tell Santa what you want for Christmas."

Kid: "Karate lessons, punching bag, Ninja suit . . ."

The biggest kid demands on Santa this year? Fashion Place Barbie for girls and Mortal Kombat III for boys.

But what about Santa's needs? Well, for one thing, Santa needs to be in shape if he is going to withstand the onslaught of kids so happy to see him that their legs won't quit jumping up and down even after getting on his lap. Either that or Santa needs some protection.

Santa also needs to think quick because some kids are more interested in information than toys. The most surprising questions on Monday were:

"Where do your reindeers go to the bathroom?"

"Do I have to eat peas and carrots?"

"Will you kiss me while I'm asleep?"

Answers: On your roof. No. Absolutely.

Santa really needs to tell parents to cool it. As evidenced by the air raid noises they make, one out of every ten kids does not want to get their picture taken while sitting on Santa's lap. What kind of memory is a snapshot of Santa and Junior's highly stressed uvula? Don't put your child through this on Christmas. For that kind of holiday trauma, wait until he or she is older and has an American Express Card.

Did Santa learn anything? You bet. In fact, every adult should try it. The clear, shining look in the eyes of children climbing onto Santa's lap says that the rest of us really ought to be doing more about nuclear weapons, bigotry, ecology, education, poverty and crime.

9-11

I must be getting old. When I first learned the extent of Tuesday's devastation at the World Trade Center, I immediately thought of my new granddaughter.

Although 2,000 miles away from the horror, my first thought was to wonder if Hallie was safe. Then I wondered about the grandchildren of others in New York City. How could anyone do something so deliberately evil to something so innocent?

This is a big switch for me. Years ago, my reaction would have been to call for an equal slaughter of the guilty, to gloat over the views from missile cameras closing in on unsuspecting targets a world away.

When Afghanistan's Taliban had the temerity to say that Osama bin Laden was not behind yesterday's attack, I was livid. We're vulnerable, not stupid. But hey, what can you possibly expect from that part of the world—a place so chaotic and unreasonable that diplomacy is a fool's errand. Why shouldn't we bomb them? Wouldn't it at least improve the world's gene pool?

It's easy to feel this way. When someone hurts you, the

first thing you want is to hurt them back. Forget the long
view, the only thing that will satisfy us is vengeance. Now.

Maybe that is why people I know to be normally reason-
able and circumspect are calling for mass retaliation. To
them, there is nothing wrong with the Middle East that nuclear weapons couldn't fix quite nicely.

Friends and even members of my family were outraged by
news footage of Palestinians dancing in the streets, exulting
over our pain and suffering: "Let's just kill 'em all."

In situations like this, the real damage isn't what evil people do to us, but what we do to ourselves in the aftermath.

At least one of the twisted goals sought by such madmen
is to initiate the rest of the world into the fellowship of hate,
to make us over in their image. In the extremity of our grief
and rage, we illogically decided that salvation lies in becoming what we loathe. I've received letters that have expressed
the following:

"The only thing these [expletive deleted] understand is
power. Kick the [deleted] out of them enough and they won't
have the nerve to try something like that again."

"These terrorists will not stop until they realize the conse-
quence of suicide attacks is the death of their mothers and
children. They are clearly willing to die for their cause. Are
they willing to let their loved ones die for the cause?
Sometimes one must act like a barbarian to stop barbarians."

" . . . where we know there is guilt, even mingled among
the innocent, we should unleash the fires of hell."

"Kill 'em all and let God sort them out."

These are not excerpts from the "Osama bin Laden Guide
to Diplomacy." These are comments from people we shop
with, work with, and with whom we go to church.

It is right to be angry and to want justice, and even to seek
the destruction of those who attack the innocent. But in doing

so, we must guard against a descent into the jungle of racism and rage.

We have been there before. After our first Pearl Harbor, we turned on ourselves in the extremity of our fear and shock. We rounded up Japanese-American citizens and put them in concentration camps.

The Middle East isn't the only birthing ground of hatred. America has its own homegrown brand of mindless terrorism. The bombing in Oklahoma City and the murders at abortion clinics are not the work of Muslim extremists.

So in the days and weeks to come, we should not presume that anyone who prays to Allah or has an olive cast to his skin is our enemy. The war against terrorism is not a struggle between races, but a fight between good and evil.

We would do well to remember that evil wears a variety of faces.

As we pick up the pieces left from the worst of our days, the goal we must share is that we never see the face of Osama bin Laden when we look into the mirror.

America has not been brought to her knees by Tuesday's insanity. If anything, we will become more united in our attitude toward those who arbitrate their demands through terror.

Some countries and certain people will soon understand what Admiral Yamamoto realized after the attack on Pearl Harbor, that a sleeping giant has been awakened.

But I hope we're careful. Somewhere in Afghanistan or Iraq, there are other new grandfathers. Just like me, all they want is for the world to make sense for their innocents.

Love
Means

Last week's vacation began at the doctor's office, where my wife was scheduled for an embarrassing procedure that Katie Couric calls "routine."

There's nothing routine about a colonoscopy. If the FBI wanted to give you one, they would have to first get a huge court order. So, to keep things light, I cracked jokes about Irene's misfortune until the lab techs came and got her.

Thirty minutes later, we found out that she has cancer. An hour later, she was in a hospital bed shot full of drugs. The following morning, they operated.

The four hours I spent waiting for her to come back from surgery set a new record on the Horrible Stuff scale. It tops the time my parachute didn't open all the way and it's worse than camping with Killer and Larry.

We brought her home after a week and a half in the hospital. The prognosis is good, if you can say that while staring down the double-barrels of chemo and radiation. She's in the next room right now, watching "Judge Judy" through a Percocet fog.

As scary as it was and is, we still find things to laugh about. She gave me a list of several women I should consider as her replacement should she die. They're all large, stingy and mean.

Today, I know exactly one thing: everything has changed. None of the old rules apply. Frankly, that's good. Most of them were based on taking our situation for granted. For example, I spent the last quarter of a century with the firm conviction that we would grow old together, have grandkids, and then—probably after something Sonny and I tried—she would get to spend my life insurance.

Because it says in our prenuptial agreement that I die first, I always assumed that she would be there. Not anymore. Over the last two weeks, I got a glimpse of what it would be like to lose her. It has been a painful education.

So far, I have learned three main things. First, that I am even stupider than previously thought, even by the people at LDS church headquarters.

A week after the surgery, I opened one of my dresser drawers and honestly thought someone had killed the sock fairy. I am learning that the washing machine does not turn itself on.

Our oldest daughter had to come over and pay the bills. I got enough money. What I don't have is clue one how it gets spread around every month. I signed forty checks and have no idea what they were for.

Did you know that dogs have to be fed every day, or that you have to put milk back in the refrigerator if you want it to stay cold?

Over the years, Irene took care of a lot of other important stuff, including what to do whenever I got fired, what I should say whenever I got pulled over, and how to help me write "sincere" letters of apology.

She's been my caretaker when I didn't deserve it, my worst enemy when I tried to get away with stuff, and my best friend even when we fought. Life without her would be impossible.

Maybe that's why stuff like this happens. It makes us re-evaluate the purpose of life. Suddenly, the plans we had for a remodeling, vacation and other things aren't as important as we thought.

Mostly, though, I think shocks like this teach us about the nature of love. Not only do you find out who you love, but how fortunate you are to have them in your life.

Someone once said that love means never having to say you're sorry. That person is an idiot. Love means being sorry that you were never sorry enough. If you're lucky, you get a chance to prove it.

After Robert Kirby wrote this article, he and his wife, Irene, we're greeted with an outpouring of concern and support from all who considered themselves close neighbors and friends, i.e., office mates, fellow churchgoers, readers of The Salt Lake Tribune *and cancer survivors from all over the country. Robert and Irene wish to acknowledge, with profound gratitude, the love that has been sent their way*

As of this writing, Irene is in remission following chemo and radiation therapy.